PTS.
THE BEAST
WITHIN

Russell Kidman, Ph.D.

PTSD The Beast Within
Copyright© 2024
Russell Kidman, Ph.D.
Contact Information:
Dr. Russell Kidman Ph.D.
www.OperationLibertyMinistry.org

Email: fourhg@hotmail.com
Web: www.OperationLibertyMinistry.org

ISBN 979-8-9896619-1-6

Publishing and Formatting Assisted by
THE OLD PATHS PUBLICATIONS, Inc.
142 Gold Flume Way
Cleveland, Georgia USA 30528
Web: www.theoldpathspublications.com
Email: TOP@theoldpathspublications.com

1.0

DEDICATION

This book is dedicated to the Men and Women of the United States Armed Services. Those who have put their lives on the line for the freedoms we hold dear as Americans.

ACKNOWLEDGMENTS

This book was reviewed by five people for feedback.

Three Veterans, two were in combat

Three Pastors, one was a Veteran

Three Civilians, two were Pastors

They were asked to answer the following questions:

Does the cover draw your attention to the book or subject?**100% Yes**

While reading did the subject matter keep your attention? **100% Yes**

> Several said they were not readers but this book kept pulling them in.

While reading did the subject matter in each chapter match the chapter head? **100% Yes**

Was this book informative on the issue of PTSD? **100% Yes**

What did you learn about PTSD from this book that

you did not know before?

> Pastor: How to help a Veteran with PTSD.

> Veteran: We are not alone in this struggle.

> Combat Veteran: It shows me how to react when I see a Veteran in distress.

> Combat Veteran: Although triggers are different the outcome of what we feel and go through is the same. We are not alone!

> Civilian: I never understood what PTSD was until I read this book; it makes me have a deeper respect for all those who have served our Country.

Would you recommend this book to a Veteran dealing with PTSD?**100% Yes**

Did this book help you understand how to help a Veteran with PTSD?**100% Yes**

(Veterans Only)

Did this book help you understand PTSD better?**100% Yes**

> Korean War Veteran: Very much, before I read this book, I thought PTSD was only a war time result, but now I realize it can be caused by other traumatic events as well.

Did this book help you personally?**100% Yes**

4

FOREWORD

One Pastor said this:

"As the pastor of New Life Independent Baptist Church I want to say that I am privileged and honored to have known and worked alongside Brother Kidman. He is truly a man with many titles such as Preacher Kidman, Sgt Kidman, Missionary Russell Kidman, Dr. Kidman and most of all my friend and brother in Christ.

I was privileged to be one of the first to proof read this book on PTSD. I want to say that before reading this book I had very little knowledge on the subject, but as I read it I found myself weeping on numerous occasions, realizing the extent of what our men and women go through after their time of serving. I have experienced firsthand in our church the effects of PTSD with Brother Kidman and now I sympathize with him and others like him with full respect of what it takes to get through these difficult times.

I want to say that I Highly recommend this book to all Veterans and those that are family, friends or caregivers for them. It will change your life and your perspective on PTSD."

Pastor Mike Whitt
New Life Ind. Baptist Church

TABLE OF CONTENTS

INTRODUCTION

No matter how you look at it, Life is made up of three main parts:

PAST
PRESENT
FUTURE

Although some would consider each of these three as separate and individual parts of one's life, the reality is that they are all connected. For instance, one's future is determined by the decisions and actions that are made in the present as the present is determined by the decisions and actions which were made in the past. To fully understand PTSD we must look at where it begins and that is in our past. Regardless of how distant and painful the past may be it is what has molded and influenced our lives; it is why we are, what we are, today. While the past may hold traumatic events from our lives, we must remember that there is both good and bad there also. We can learn how to use those experiences to better our life in the present which in turn will directly affect our future.

During basic training I had to work extra hard conditioning my body to meet the required Army physical fitness standards. I was so out of shape that I experienced pain in places I didn't even know I had places. Some days I was in so much pain that I wondered how I could go on, but as time went on the pain grew less and less until I noticed that physically I had grown stronger. What once was painful became tolerable and eventually enjoyable. The pains of our past must be exercised in the same way, like our bodies during PT, until what once hurt us, actually helps us through our daily lives.

Yes, PTSD can actually become an asset instead of the burden of depression that has caused so many of our fellow Veterans to take their own life. First of all understand that EVERYONE has a past and not everything in that past was harmful, but too often we focus on one part of our past instead of the whole picture.

It was a happy day when we arrived back in Baumholder Germany from Desert Storm, but the carnage of our lives and marriages had yet to come. In the Army, we had trained and prepared for WAR however we were given no training or preparation for what would lay ahead after we came home. I had always been a happy go lucky type of person that some considered a clown, but all of a sudden I regularly faced depression, and extreme hardships dealing with sights and sounds that reminded me of the war. After leaving the Military things only digressed to the point that I had difficulty working with others and keeping a steady job. I hated being around large groups of people, especially if I didn't know them. Some accused me of being extremely paranoid because I was always checking my six or I would get anxious around strangers and foreigners.

Every aspect of this effected those around me, especially my family who experienced my distancing and rage but did not understand why I wanted to be alone or why I had such a "short fuse" or why I was just staring into nothing. In 1995 I met a Korean War Veteran who took an interest in helping me and my family because he understood what was going on. His intervention definitely changed my outlook on life and probably saved our marriage as he helped me focus on my family instead of my pain. Although our lives have since taken us in different directions, I am forever in his debt for his friendship and compassion. Several years later the LORD called us to travel and Minister to our Troops with the same compassion and friendship once shown to us. Since 2006 I have been helping others the way that Korean War Veteran helped me. This booklet was written so that this knowledge can reach thousands of souls that I may never meet.

There are some things that we must know from our past that are directly affecting our present and will eventually affect our future. The term Post Traumatic Stress Disorder (PTSD) has been widely used, and in some cases misused for an advantage. We desire to look into the things that have occurred in one's life that could have influenced the current issues and help that individual learn these "triggers" to better lead a more normal life.

Dr. Russell Kidman Ph.D

P—THE PAST

I grew up in what most would consider a middle class home in the 1960's as a country boy. We lived on a farm, but did not farm it ourselves. Throughout my early years we had horses and goats from time to time and our neighbor had hogs. We learned early that you didn't want to get caught by the bore or even a few sow's either. At times I would cut through the hog pen until once I got caught by an old sow that tried to chew my foot off. My horse had a habit of running real fast then stopping on a dime and ducking its head so you would go sailing over on your backside. My first dog bite was while I was trying to pay our neighbor for a dozen eggs. Good thing I didn't have the eggs in hand yet so after a little cleanup of my arm they sent me home with a free dozen of eggs for mom. Everything in our life today is there because of our PAST, everything we consider good and everything we consider bad, from our earliest memories as a child to yesterdays traffic jam.

There are many aspects to my past including my time in the military. A friend of mine once commented that I had PTSD long before I entered the military because of the many things that happened to me early in my life. By the time I was a teenager my parents had been divorced for years and then I was abandoned and homeless at 16 years old. Throughout my adolescence and teen years I was shot three times, stabbed three times, fell over a twenty foot cliff, had my tent torn down by a mountain lion (while I was in it), and on April 17th 1979 I was riding my motorcycle out of town when a semi turned in front of me and we collided, all that was before I ever set foot in the military. Although chapters could be written about each of these events and many others, they were shared to say this: you don't have to have been in combat to have issues with PTSD. However for the focus of this book we will be directing our thoughts dealing with the issues faced by our brothers and sisters who have signed that blank check up to and including their life in any of the branches of our Military.

My Father was a WWII combat veteran and even though he did not want any of his sons to join the military three of us did and the fourth one served our country in Fire and Rescue retiring as a Battalion Fire Chief. Like two of my brothers I too felt a deep desire to serve our country and that is why I tried several different branches of service before getting accepted into the U.S. Army. The Air Force kicked me out because I was four pounds overweight and the Navy, well they accused me of fraudulent enlistment because I had told the Air Force about sleep walking at age thirteen but forgot to mention it when I tried to join the Navy. It had been nine years since it happened and four years since I mentioned it to anyone so I had simply forgotten about it. After being kicked out of the Navy I was angry but three years later, once again I got the bug to serve our country. I was in college studying engineering when I went to talk to the recruiter who offered me the GI Bill, worth $25,000.00 to help with my college and a bonus of another $25,000.00 doubling my GI Bill if I would sign up in combat arms. I was given the speech about how I could take college classes while in the military and they would pay for them which would allow me to use my GI Bill for further education once I left the military. It all sounded good and already having a desire to serve it didn't take much to sign me up. I scored a 96 on the ASVAB tests and could have had nearly any job in the Army but I was told that as a 13E Fire Direction Specialist I would be doing tasks similar to what I was studying in college. Just a side note here; nearly every one of my comrades in FDC were told the same story and were also studying engineering like me when they enlisted. Yeah, about that… nothing we did was even close to engineering!

FORT SILL OK

There were hundreds of us civilians who showed up one day in Lawton, OK and boarded a bus to Fort Sill for basic training. At the welcome station everything seemed pretty laid back but then we were taken across the tracks to the training area and all Hell broke loose. The "Shark Attack" was on and basic had begun. Although much of basic training was physically challenging the biggest part to me was the mental breaking down of civilians into a cohesive unit and my first experiences of the "Brotherhood" that comes from serving.

I had grown up leaning to shoot but in the Army my marksmanship went from just hitting the target to grouping shots within the size of a quarter. Whether a target was fifty meters up to three hundred meters away it was going down. I qualified EXPERT on the rifle, on the machine gun, and throwing grenades on the Grenade range. I had lost all my excess weight, was becoming physically strong and believed I was now a lean, mean fighting machine ready for warfare.

FORT HOOD TX

This was my first duty station with 1stBattalion 3rd Field Artillery 2nd Armored Division. My first duty assignment was advance party for Alpha Battery 1st Platoon FDC. Since I was already going to be in advance party I was also made the driver for our Gunnery Sgt who was in charge of that group. Ft Hood was the first Army base to change from WWII jeeps to the new Humvees. Including the two driving instructors, I became the 4th person on Ft Hood licensed to drive one of these and was assigned a model 1038 Humvee with winch to lead our advance party. Working directly for the Gunny Sgt, while also learning my MOS had some great benefits and helped me move up through the ranks quickly. As a PFC I had proven my abilities by taking over the section during a field training mission when both my Staff Sgt and Corporal became ill and had to be taken back to the rear for medical reasons. By the time I was in the Army eleven months I had already been promoted to E4 Specialist and at fifteen months I was sent to the E5 Board and passed with 190 points out of 200 possible. My Battalion Command Sergeant Major McNair began to take an interest in me early on in my career. He would often request me for Battalion special duty for his office. As just a PFC at first I was intimidated by his rank and position but quickly learned that he was interested in developing leaders that one  day would be able to replace him when he was gone. Once I reported to his office properly he quickly sat me down at a desk and handed me a book, which I was required to read unless he asked me to run an errand. When I would finish he would quiz me on what I learned from my reading and hand me another book to read. These books were on multiple subjects of which two were leadership and tactics that he wanted me to learn. However one of the greatest things I learned from CSM McNair was to laugh at myself and things that would happen in the military. He was the NCOIC of my promotion board, for which he had the last question of the day. I already knew the question he would ask and the answer was going to be who was playing in the World Series, but instead of just asking me the question he first asked if I keep up with sports or not. I had been too busy learning my MOS to keep up with sports so I answered No Sergeant Major. Therefore, he decided to change the question, while he kept it in the subject of current events. He asked what important event took place in December of the previous year. I couldn't think of anything that I had recently studied about. I asked him to rephrase the question so he did, "On Dec 27th 1986 an event took place that forever changed the world, what was that event?" I thought about world events, military events then finally told him I did not know but would make sure I found out and would never forget it after that. CSM McNair, sitting on a Military Board, started laughing hysterically as he pounded his fist on the table. He was laughing so hard that he fell off of his chair onto the floor and by now all the other Senior NCO's were laughing and pounding the table too. I was trying to maintain my "Military Appearance" by staying at the position of Attention while seated but, the laughing just kept getting worse. Finally the CSM pulled his head back above the table, still laughing, and said to me "does your wife know you don't know when your anniversary is?" and continued to laugh hysterically while getting back into his chair. After that day whenever CSM McNair saw me he would holler at me "Hey Kidman"... "Have you told your wife yet, that you forgot your anniversary?" While playing racquetball one day with my XO and 1st Sgt, CSM McNair showed up as the fourth person. When he served the ball and I tried to return it, I accidentally hit him in the back of the head with the ball. He looked at me and said "you serve" so I did and he purposely hit me in the back of the head with the ball as he said "now that we got that over with, can we just play racquetball as men!" There are many other stories about CSM McNair and his influence on my life and military career. The most important thing that I learned from him was that he was a man just like me with a few more stripes. He taught me to take life as it comes and find the humor in it even if it bothers others. I lost track of him when I PCS'ed to Germany in 1988 and only recently learned that he passed away in 2018. CSM McNair, I have never once forgotten my Wedding Anniversary and for that I am most Thankful.

BAUMHOLDER GERMANY

This was my second duty station with 2nd Battalion 29th FA 8th Infantry Division. It was here that I became the primary computer operator for 2nd Platoon FDC in Alpha Btry. Through various field training  exercises I further honed my skills even though I had not officially been promoted to sergeant yet I still served in that capacity of leadership. The FDC chief in 1st platoon was new to artillery even though that was his primary MOS at enlistment. He spent his first six years running track for the U.S. Army Track Team and even competed in the Olympics twice. When he was no longer competitive he was sent to a sixty day training school for FDC training to learn some maintenance and operation of the radios. He had not come up through the ranks in this MOS and it showed up especially when he went to the field where he always had an excuse of why his equipment wasn't working. Twice I was put in his section during ARTEP to make sure the section and our Battery both passed the tests required for combat.

THE CHALLENGE

We had a new FDO (Fire Direction Officer) in our unit whose job was to verify our firing data that it was "Safe" and wouldn't hit friendly troops. This new FDO had graduated from West Point and was very arrogant, especially towards enlisted personal. He told me I was terrible at my job and that he could do my job better than I could, so he challenged me to a shoot-out of artillery. We were a self-propelled 155mm cannon unit shooting high explosive rounds that has a bursting radius of around 150 meters. According to Army standards once FDC received a call for fire we had a twenty second mission time to compute the data and send it down to the guns (cannons). The FDO went first firing four guns, one at a time so the observer could report the accuracy of each round. His mission time was 1 minute 4 seconds, nowhere near required mission time. As each round impacted the target area the observer called them back over the radio. The closest to the target of his four rounds sent down range was 187 meters, a complete miss!

Now it was my turn! Mission time 6 seconds (my average was 11 seconds) and here is the observers report for each round fired one round at a time.

1st round – Steel on target
2nd round – Steel on target
3rd round – Steel on target
4th round – within five meters of target

I called the observer back and said what do you mean five meters on the last round, he explained that a "smoke round" had been fired in-between the 3rd and 4th rounds and it covered the target so the best he could estimate was within five meters, that I could accept. During the next few months I had several confrontations with this FDO as he began setting me up for a court martial because I had embarrassed him so much.

On another field training exercise this same officer ordered me to fire a round after range shutdown and I refused. When he tried to hit the fire button on my computer I turned it off. He then computed the data himself and gave a voice command to fire the round and it was observed safe, however we were the only unit on the range that had not yet reported to range control to acknowledge range shutdown. Another unit fired a round and shrapnel from that round hit Range Control Headquarters. We were held responsible for this because that lieutenant refused to acknowledge range control that we were no longer shooting live rounds. As the primary computer operator everything pointed to me for the fault.

Rear the Piece, Face the Piece, Fall In, came over the radio as the investigation into what happened started. Range Control showed up demanding all our documentation and records of when and where we fired that day. They searched my computer for previously fired data that gets stored and found nothing. Our Captain was there questioning everyone in the section. The Battalion Commander was there questioning everything and everyone. The post commander showed up with smoke rolling out from his collar yelling at the Battalion Commander and our unit Commander. If you've never been through something like that, trust me it's the last place you ever want to be!

Finally after hours upon hours of questioning everyone involved from the lowest rank to the highest rank my CO called me aside and asked what really happened. The CO said he was asking me because he knew I would tell the truth and put an end to this madness of inspections and investigations. I told him exactly what had happened and how I tried to stop it from even taking place to begin with. Within minutes after speaking to the CO it was all over with and everyone was leaving. The next morning the FDO officer was given a Division Letter of Reprimand ending his career. He could serve out the rest of his current enlistment but after that his status as an officer was revoked and he would ETS from the Army.

FINALLY AN NCO

In June of 1988 I was promoted to E5 Sgt and began

my life as a Jr. NCO. In January of 1989 I was assigned to take 1st Platoon's M577A2 track vehicle out on reforger in the middle of January. The track was not well maintained and had many "Deadline items" that I had to first get fixed before we could even leave the motor pool, one of which was the crew heater that only ran occasionally. The outside temperatures were around zero degrees Fahrenheit so heat was critical. This was my first "command" if you will and I was told that the XO had all the dispatches but it seemed he did not have mine. The harder I tried to make things right the worse my situation got. That FDO had now become the XO and he wasn't working alone he had help from several privates that did not like me because since my promotion I was the one who reported them AWOL from duty as Sgt of the Guard. They ended up getting busted and blamed me for it so helping the XO bring charges against me in their eyes was a good thing. During lunch break that day the XO approached me with several other Officers where there was over sixty other NCO's and enlisted as he placed me at Attention and began to reprimand me with the 26 charges he had manufactured against me. As he read them off I drew back my fist to punch him dead in the face and that is when he added assaulting an officer to my charges. Years later a retired 1st Sgt told me I should have just hit him because it would have still been the same charge and I would have felt better!

TROUBLE FROM WEST POINT

Now that he was the XO he decided to turn things around on me. He made up all these charges and then put me on a 30-60-90 counseling, meaning every thirty days I would be counseled by him with a list of things I need to improve or he was going to see that I stood before a court marshal. I did everything he asked even improved my pt scores and yet nothing ever seemed to be enough. Finally at the 90 day counseling session he announced that I was incompetent as an NCO and it was his intention to see my stripes removed from me and insure I spent time in Leavenworth KS for my other crimes he had charged me with. Up to this point in the military I was known as a "By the book' NCO and was looking forward to staying in the military as a career. As I left his office I passed the 1st Sgt's office and I shouted "THAT'S IT I QUIT!" Top (1st Sgt) came out of his office and grabbed me by the sleeve dragging me into his office. He sat me in a chair and asked what was going on for me to make such a contrary statement to the kind of soldier I was. I had watched this officer get our previous 1st Sgt relieved of command. I had watched him take on senior NCO's with the only purpose of ruining their lives and he succeeded. No one was standing up against him for me because he had done this in the past. How was I a buck Sgt going to get past this mess that was started because he got embarrassed? I told Top that I probably should just go wrap my car around a tree somewhere and that is when he sent me to see an Army shrink; the reason, because I had threatened suicide.

CHARGES DISAPPEAR

Top handed me my 201 personal file and asked if he could trust me to bring it back and I said yes of course. I spent several hours with the shrink who basically said I was under too much stress and needed to be removed from that officers command. He didn't understand that it doesn't happen that way in combat arms. I returned to the unit with my 201 file in hand looking for someone to turn it into but no one was there. Top wasn't there, the CO wasn't there, Platoon Sgts and Platoon Leaders were all gone. No one was on the CQ desk the place was deserted so I headed for the door to take it to the BN Headquarters personal office. On my way out I met up with my Platoon Sgt who asked me what was going on, so I updated him about the whole situation. He said he would take my 201 file, so I handed it to him and began to walk away when he called "Sgt Kidman come here". I turned around and came back to him as he opened my 201 file and began rummaging through it looking for something. Ah he said as he found what he was looking for and began taking pages out of my 201 file and handing them to me. One after another he removed all the charges in my file and placed them all in my hands. He closed the file and asked me a question "Sgt Kidman did you remove anything from your 201 file?" No Sgt I replied and he said "correct answer, have a nice day!" and sent me on my way.

The next day the XO called me into his office and asked me if I took anything out of my 201 file when I had it in my possession yesterday. I could honestly say NO SIR I did not! He asked who I gave it to and what they did with it so I said you will have to ask the Platoon Sgt because I turned it into him. The XO was furious, all his plans were gone and he didn't have backups. His plan to destroy me for embarrassing him was ruined and I was a free NCO. The XO set his sights on Platoon Sgt Daughtry because he took the heat for me and was eventually relieved of duty a few months later. That was a good thing because he was made our supply Sgt just before we deployed to Desert Storm and he was just like Radar on Mash. He could get anything, it might take a lot of trading of things we didn't need but, he could get it and that is the kind of supply Sgt we needed in Desert Storm.

Oh what ever happened to that officer you ask? He was taken from the gun line and put in headquarters as a junior officer because Battalion knew there were too many looking forward to seeing him in a war zone and giving him a dose of real life injected by a 5.56mm syringe! He was promotable to Captain when all this business took place between us and even with a letter of reprimand he was going to see captain but never see Major. Shortly after we returned to Germany I saw him one day and saluted him as he walked by. He had just been promoted to captain that day so I respectfully said "Congratulations on your LAST promotion sir" He didn't like that very much but there wasn't anything he could do about it as he was no longer in my chain of command.

MY LEADERSHIP EXAMPLE

Through all this I learned it is not about how good you are or how well you are known but about whom you know. Platoon Sgt Daughtry and I knew each other back at Ft Hood where we were in sister units before coming there. He knew that the only thing that could be taken from him was his command status, and that wouldn't affect his retirement at all. On the other hand I was looking down a very long dark path to prison and a bad discharge for something I didn't do. His example became my purpose as an NCO to always defend and look out for the well being of my soldiers regardless of the situation or how it might affect me personally. Later on in Desert Storm this would be put to the test as one of the soldiers who helped set me up with that lieutenant was now under my care and needed to go home to help save his brother's life, which had been injured in a gasoline explosion. He had received eight Red Cross letters from home yet command said he could not go home. This time I stood up for him and made sure he went home to help his brother. It cost me a huge butt chewing and some pretty nasty details but in the end it was all worth it. The second thing that came out of these experiences with the XO was that I became untouchable at least in my mind. I no longer took anything from anyone regardless of their rank.I became ever more hard-core as an NCO than ever before. Now I had a clearer understanding of the responsibilities of my position. I made it my intention to live up to the NCO Creed and be the Best NCO I could be, by gaining the respect of those under me and helping to guide them through their career in the Army. I led by example, not fear, I didn't ask anything of them I wasn't willing to do myself. This wasn't always the easy way but it turned out to be the best way to lead men in war.

NCO CREED

No one is more professional than I. I am a noncommissioned officer, a leader of Soldiers. As a noncommissioned officer, I realize that I am a member of a time honored corps, which is known as "The Backbone of the Army". I am proud of the Corps of noncommissioned officers and will at all times conduct myself so as to bring credit upon the Corps, the military service and my country regardless of the situation in which I find myself. I will not use my grade or position to attain pleasure, profit, or personal safety.

Competence is my watchword. My two basic responsibilities will always be uppermost in my mind—accomplishment of my mission and the welfare of my Soldiers. I will strive to remain technically and tactically proficient. I am aware of my role as a noncommissioned officer. I will fulfill my responsibilities inherent in that role. All Soldiers are entitled to outstanding leadership; I will provide that leadership. I know my Soldiers and I will always place their needs above my own. I will communicate consistently with my Soldiers and never leave them uninformed. I will be fair and impartial when recommending both rewards and punishment.

Officers of my unit will have maximum time to accomplish their duties; they will not have to accomplish mine. I will earn their respect and confidence as well as that of my Soldiers. I will be loyal to those with whom I serve; seniors, peers, and subordinates alike. I will exercise initiative by taking appropriate action in the absence of orders. I will not compromise my integrity, nor my moral courage. I will not forget, nor will I allow my comrades to forget that we are professionals, noncommissioned officers, leaders!

One year after being promoted to Sergeant my section Chief recommended that I be sent to the next promotion board E6 Staff Sgt. Our Platoon Sergeant never allowed me to go because in his words, "you are a Christian and will not go to war to kill the enemy". His theory was based upon one of the Ten Commandments which states "thou shalt not kill". The word "kill" used therein means to murder and I understand the difference between war and murder but evidently he didn't. Murder is personal between two individuals and yes we are commanded not to murder. However, war is corporate, as in one Nation against another Nation. I began showing my platoon sergeant, from the Bible, how God has used one nation to judge another nation through the act of war and those actions are not attributive to the individual. Even with all that evidence he would not recommend me to the promotion board. My Section Chief knew I was ready for advancement and it was his intention to send me again after the Platoon Sgt left our unit but no sooner had he left than Saddam Hussein, sent his troops into Kuwait City and we were called upon to go to war, my promotion would have to wait.

Throughout each of these events in my past I learned something that is now a part of my present and affecting my future. However, I wouldn't have made it through most of the issues I faced without someone else intervening on my behalf. A slogan I picked up many years ago is this: "Others Lord others let this my motto be, that I may live for others, more than I live for me".

T—THE TRAUMA

It would be impossible to document every aspect of PTSD for one simple reason. Why, well my Lieutenant once put it this way; *"there is no normal reaction to combat".* No two Veterans are going to react the same way. While we may have many similarities, in the end our reactions are different. Therefore the things that affected me personally, or many of the Veterans I have ministered to for decades, may not be your issue but they are the "Price of Freedom"! Someone had to pay and this book is for those of us who did!

THE NOISE OF WAR

Certain noises can adversely affect the state of any Veteran who has been subjected to the sounds of war. For some this could be a high pitched whistle or tone, many of us are dealing with hearing loss from the loudness of war, so what seems perfectly normal for you may in fact be excruciating to the Veteran. For me this is a personal issue because in the operations of my primary MOS I had to monitor five radio's, one of which was digital. I was so in tune that I could tell by the sound of the digital signal if the information was coming to us or another unit. Even during times I was supposed to be sleeping after I awoke, I would know who was talking to whom on which radio and what they had been talking about. Today there is a constant ringing in my head that distorts nearly everything that I hear and even affects my relationships with family and friends.

Where do these sounds come from? It could be from anything, but usually it is from something mechanical that is not normally supposed to make any sound, yet it is now squealing or making a high pitch sound. This has happened in stores where their AC unit was not functioning correctly, or the squeak of a door as it is opened. Once we were traveling and just as we passed through the tunnel from West Virginia into Virginia our heater blower motor started whistling. This was in the middle of the winter, but regardless it had to be stopped, so I simply turned the fan off and only had a minimal amount of heat enough to keep the front window clear. You may think that was extreme but the sound of that constant whistle and the ringing in my ears combined, was so unbearable I was willing to be cold instead. Yes, every little bit we would stop and I'd let my wife turn the heater motor back on and warm things up while I went for a short walk to get away from that sound. Not everyone may have an issue with things like this but for those of us who do; it is just life after the war.

Then there are those loud noises, you know like fireworks, car back-firing, or simply someone firing weapons for no apparent reason. When I was a kid my dad would never go to the fireworks on Independence Day. He would take us there and tell us when he would pick us up afterwards. Our town had the best display of any around and we enjoyed it but I always wondered why dad would not come. He was very patriotic and a Combat Veteran from World War

II. When asked he would just say something like, "that's not for me". Shortly after I got out of military I had my first experience with fireworks and it wasn't a good one. I began seeing the tanks that had surrounded us as they were being blown up by our Abrams tanker friends. The smell of gun powder was everywhere and with that I could still smell the burning flesh and see them dying all over again. My family did not understand just like I did not understand my Dad years before.

Well one would say just be like your Dad and don't go to the fireworks, and that is true so I don't. However, there are times that we have attended events that we did not know they were going to set off fireworks and, well, here we go again. It doesn't have to be fireworks; it could be someone just firing a weapon without the Veteran being aware of it. This has happened on several occasions in my life and there was no ill intent but none the less it drastically affected me during that time frame and for many days afterwards. Those are the drastic examples of loud noise, but it can be as simple as a door slamming or books being dropped on the floor. In restaurants I have been triggered by the accidental dropping of plates or pans in the kitchen. Then there is the old "pop'n john", that's what I call vehicles that backfire. Our neighbor when I was a kid had a John Deer tractor and it would always backfire when he started it. If you've ever been around one of those old tractors, you would know exactly what I mean.

In general it doesn't even have to be all that loud, but it is the unexpected noise that jars us into that previous life of war. The point to understand here is that one thing leads to another. It may be that the "noise" that triggers us today in this particular setting, may be manageable tomorrow in another setting. Although this "noise" may be the trigger in an event, it has a lot to do with the surroundings complementing that "noise" that causes an unwanted reaction. We are trained to listen and identify sounds "noise" and there is no telling what sound or "noise" will affect us today. It could be a screaming child in a store that alerts us or the behavior of a group of individuals that displays a threatening posture or demeanor. Then the sound happens and all this together is the fullness of what we call the trigger.

When we go out in public we cannot control the noises around us, and this is why so many Combat Veterans do not like to be involved in social events especially in large crowds. *Define large: more than a squad...(five or more).* Much like the military where I was familiar with all the noises of my comrades and equipment, today I am the same way with my vehicles, home, and friends, I am familiar with the "normal noises" of life. When something happens outside those "normal noises" it affects me by drawing my attention to that noise. I have to make sure it is not a threat to my family or myself, in any way shape or form. Then and only then can one begin the process of standing down and getting back to "normal".

THE OTHER WORLD

To some this is what you may call dreaming, but to the veteran it is another world. Once I had returned from combat my Dad finally opened up to me about his "Night Terrors" (Dreams). I can only suppose he did this to try to help me understand what was happening to me as well. To me it is like living in two separate and different worlds. The peculiar thing about these dreams is people I did not know until after the war can appear in these dreams during the war. This is going to sound really out there, but please give a little grace. They are so vivid that at times it is difficult to know which world is real and which one is a dream. Sometimes my family members at their current ages are in these dreams but the setting is during the time of the war. If someone were to be observing me it would appear that I am sleeping but when I awake I'm worn out from all the action and fighting throughout the night. Often when I awake from one of these "dreams" I have to check to see where I woke up at. Each person has to develop something that helps them to identify if they are still in the "dream" or back in reality. Once that can be checked and verified it is a relief to know it was only another "night terror". Sometimes when I awake the "rage of war" is so strong that I'm still angry for hours that day. It is during those times that I read the 23rd Psalm, written by King David and personally I believe it was how he dealt with his PTSD from all the wars and fighting he had done throughout his life. We will talk more about that later in another chapter, but suffice it to say that it really helps me calm back down from a night of war.

These dreams are not limited to just a "nightmare", but on many occasions I have actually acted them out physically. Of course I was not aware of this but I have been told by family that "I was doing it again last night". We have dealt with many Veterans who have had these experiences in such a drastic way that they have left their family home and found another place to live. This is not because they don't love their family or want to be around them, but because we become afraid of what we will do to them while acting out one of the "night terror dreams". Their spouse doesn't understand what is going on and becomes afraid of the one they love. In the many times of my life that I have acted out my "night terror dreams" only once has my actions resulted in a member of my family getting injured. The following morning when you are told what you did it horrifies you! When the very people you would die to protect, your family, are injured it rips your heart out. Then this fear of hurting the ones you love turns into rage as you become angry with yourself for something you had no control over. Again this is why so many Veterans choose to live separate from their families. This adds stress to the home and marriage and is a leading cause of why so many marriages of Veterans end in divorce.

This is seen by most civilians as an extreme reaction

to a "bad dream", but they do not understand that we know our capabilities and fear what could happen if we don't take these extreme measures. I have known many families that have done this and after years of work and dedication they have been able to reunite into one household. On the other hand I have also seen some regress into almost a hermit mindset, not wanting to see or hear from anyone, even family. This wanting to be isolated is not good and often leads to depression and suicide. No matter how difficult it is to live with or around your Veteran don't allow them to ever feel they are alone against the world. This is when they become most susceptible to becoming one of the twenty two a day that take their own life.

THE RAGGING LUNATIC

Well that's what I've been told it comes across as when the "rage of war" come out of us. There is a "rage" that builds up inside of you once you have seen combat. When triggered it's like a beast has been unleashed within you that is often quite contrary to your normal character. I'm not really sure where it comes from other than to say it is part of the "fight or flight" mechanism God put within us. When we become threatened and reach that point where we would rather fight than flee, it is usually accompanied by an overwhelming rush of anger as the adrenaline flows though our body. This "rage" or anger pushes us to be more brutal and savage than our aggressor in order to survive the attack and be victorious in battle.

After coming home this "rage" takes on a new role in

our lives in a way that is not really acceptable to society. Even in the most humble of people this "rage" can come out when we are tested or questioned for no apparent reason. This can be answering some one's question over and over. This repetition inflates the "rage" as we don't understand why our answer is not sufficient. It can be when we have to complete the same task over and over because what is suppose to work, all of a sudden doesn't work. The computer keeps freezing up, or the printer won't work today but did yesterday. It is usually something little and insignificant, but each time we have to repeat the process the repetition of the action brings out that "rage". I have been asked how I was so happy just a few minutes ago, but now I'm flying off the handle just because I couldn't get something to work right? For many years I had no answer for this problem and because I had no answer that would make me even angrier. There had to be a reason I was all of a sudden so angry that I'd rather smash this device than try to fix it.

One of the things about the military is that there is usually a protocol on how something is done. Although there may have been a dozen different ways the job could have been done, it was done based upon the unit protocol every time. During combat I almost shot three officers that were running towards my fighting position. I gave them a command to "Halt" and they kept running. The second time I said "Halt or I'll fire", this time they stopped in their tracks. It was about 0400 hours in the morning and we were expecting an attack, when we heard a shot fired and then these three started running at our location. Once stopped, I gave a challenge phrase and they gave the appropriate response so I could allow them to advance one at a time to be recognized. The first one was my Captain; the second one was my Executive Officer and the third one was my Fire Direction Officer that I worked with every day. He asked me why I threatened to fire on them and I simply responded "Who broke protocol sir, you or me?" That protocol saved their lives that day because it was obeyed.

There is a process in life and when that process gets interrupted it breaks the protocol we have set in our minds. This in turn opens up our memory to the dangers of protocol not being followed and it becomes frustrating to say the least. This broken protocol is referenced as a threat and the "rage of war" needed to conquer the situation starts to show its ugly face. The problem with this is obvious and that is the fact that my computer not working properly is not a life threatening event. For years my wife would try to correct me when this would happen and that only resulted in furthering the "rage" (like pouring gasoline on an open fire). I still get "the look" but she has learned to just be quiet and let me realize how pathetic I really sound shouting at a computer or phone or whatever.

THE MEDICINE CABINET

This is otherwise called self medicating. To some they

are just a drunk pathetic excuse for a human being, but in reality they are hurting and need help. Drug and alcohol addictions are most common in Combat Veterans because they are trying to medicate a pain that never goes away. Everything we have discussed up to this point contributes to this issue in so many Veterans' lives.

After receiving our orders to deploy to Desert Storm I called my WWII Veteran Dad for advice. He was very clear on what he said and it has helped me more now than at that time. First he said read Psalm 91. This scripture gave me a peace that helped me be the NCO I needed to be no matter how nervous I was or how scary the situation, there was a promise from God that I was His and He would watch over me. The second piece of advice from Dad was this; "when you go to war you are the KING of BATTLE, but when you come home you become the WHORE of the nation"! Dad couldn't have been more right on both accounts. We had spent years training for "war", playing "war games" learning our strengths and weaknesses, learning the same of our enemies. Our capabilities had grown as we matured in the ranks of the military as well as our physical being. The slogan of my unit was "Battle Ready Sir", and we said that every time we saluted an officer whether he was with our unit or not. We had practiced and practiced over and over so we knew our job as well as the person above and below us. We did everything we could to prepare for war and when it was time we were ready.

We did our jobs so well that when it was all over with we were given a presidential citation for the most precise artillery in the history of warfare.

However coming home was a different story. Nothing was done to prepare us for what lie ahead in our lives. There were no debriefing classes only a pat on the back and have a nice life. No one ever mentioned anything about PTSD; the noises of battle, the night terrors, the rage or pain that would follow from all of these building up inside us after we came home. It was supposed to be a good time back with family but we had changed so much that our families didn't recognize us as the same person. Well that is kind of true because the person who left for war never really comes home. The same body and name maybe, but we are forever changed mentally, physically and spiritually. We are dealing with things that we never knew existed and society just thinks we are broken beyond repair so they cast us out. Many Veterans have a very difficult time readjusting to civilian life and therefore find it difficult to hold down a job or keep their family together. All this takes a toll on the Veteran as they get more and more discouraged and depressed as life tumbles out of protocol or control.

The solution that too many find is the drug world where pills or powder will take them away from all the pain associated with their time in combat. For others it starts as just a beer or two each night. Both ways it ends up controlling their life and the reason their life is falling apart. On top of the PTSD issues they already have now, they've added an addiction that takes their time, money and personality away from them and their family. Many end up alone and on the streets, homeless and miserable. However, as much as I hate to say so, this self medicating keeps them in a state of mind sufficient enough that the thought of suicide is usually not pursued. Sadly this life style will cause them more health issues in the long run and eventually lead to a horrible death unless intervention is possible.

I have been through many traumatic things in my life and through each one I have found a greater strength to push forward each day. We must purposely make a choice each day how we are going to let any traumatic events in our lives effect us or those around us.

S—EFFECTS OF STRESS

Stress comes from the fight between mind & body that takes place during each episode of PTSD. When I learned to play the guitar it was explained to me that as my body learned "muscle memory" for each cord I wouldn't have to think of where to place my fingers they would just go there as I saw the cord progression of a song. In many ways the training we received from basic and throughout our military career was building "muscle memory" for combat. We begin to respond to situations based upon our training without even thinking about it, it just happens.

In combat we need that "muscle memory" to take effect to survive the battles each day. However in civilian life that same "muscle memory" is now not needed, but there none the less and comes across to civilians as a burst of rage that is out of control. This causes stress between our mind and body reactions to an event. Our body is in full "muscle memory" mode preparing us for battle while our mind is evaluating the situation and not seeing a military threat or action taking place. This is why we seem to be distressed or anxious when in public places around people we do not know. The mind sees the calm civilian situation, but the noise, sudden movement or flash of light triggers our body to prepare for combat.

REDEPLOYMENT

My entire unit was ordered to attend a redeployment

briefing just before we deployed home from Saudi Arabia. This briefing was given by the Divarty Chaplain supposedly to help us with our transition back home. We were in KKMC and it was hot, I mean Saudi desert hot, but we had become used to it by now. There was a GP medium tent set up for chapel where we all gathered together expecting the usual long dry Army briefings we had grown accustomed to. The Chaplain started as one would expect him to with a prayer and quote of the day. This didn't take very long and then he spent just a few more minutes on the schedule for our redeployment back to Germany to be with our families. Finally he got to the main subject which we were all looking forward too of reintegration back with our families. One would think as we did to expect something "spiritual" from a Chaplain but his whole message to us was over in just a few minutes. The basic emphasis of the message was that we had been gone a long time and had probably done things because we were lonely. Well he continued so has Mamma back home so just forgive each other and move on. Yep, that was about it, we all walked away from that briefing in disbelief and some of us very angry. Let's just say it did not have the effect he had planned but actually just the opposite.

What should have been a briefing on PTSD and its effects on us and our family, turned out to be just an insult of how he believed our wives' had acted and it enraged nearly everyone that was married. This added stress made the reunion with our families difficult as his absurd suggestion was in the back of our minds regardless of how much we trusted our wife. It became one of the first subjects that my wife and I discussed behind closed doors but the suggestion still haunted both of us for years later, until we both agreed that it was foolishness and once again fully trusted each other. This wasn't easy but it was necessary to move our relationship forward. However it wouldn't have been possible without the Lord Jesus Christ in the middle of our marriage. We had misplaced our focus on a perverted notion, which drew us apart, but once we put our focus back on the Lord this helped us overcome false suggestions even if they were given by a supposed "spiritual leader" Chaplain. For many of my comrades who did not believe in God they had no hope and most ended up allowing that suggestion to destroy their home. This was just the first stage of stress that we would follow that no one ever said anything about, we had to figure it out on our own.

FLASHBACKS

It was only a few days after returning from Saudi Arabia that I attended Church services off post at Grace Baptist Church in Baumholder Germany. This was our Church where we regularly attended every week when I wasn't out training. Everyone there was either in the Army or Retired Military. They had become a family to us and were a critical part of taking care of my family while I was deployed. I was excited to see them and worship with them again but that is not how the day went. Just a few clicks away there was a German machine-gun range and in the middle of services they opened fire on that range and I can only tell you what others told me happened. I dropped to the ground and low crawled out the door to a vantage point where I could secure the front entrance of the building. While this was disruptive to the services our Pastor, a Vietnam Combat Veteran told everyone to leave me alone and went right back to preaching. Out on the perimeter, I noticed someone slid up beside me. They were also in the prone position and asked what was going on. I briefed them of the situation as I saw it. This person was also a Vietnam Combat Veteran and he gently said to me "Russ, you are home and safe it's just a machine gun range run by the German Military." I remember looking at him and realizing where I was and felt like a fool. He and Pastor met with me after everyone else had left and tried to explain that things like this would happen but it isn't something to be embarrassed about because it is normal.

Normal, what was that, I wondered my lieutenant had told me there is no normal in combat. This was just the first of the experiences I would endure. Just a few days later a close couple from the Church threw a welcome home party for me and invited a lot of the men and their families from the Church. When my family and I arrived I found a place to sit and someone turned on the TV where a Civil War movie was playing. I began to weep and shake until one of the men in a picket line had their head taken off by a cannon ball. Again I can only tell you what was told to me, as I ran out of their apartment and was found two and a half hours later in the basement shaking, trembling and weeping. I had no idea why I was reacting this way or what was going on. My friend tried to apologize over and over even though I didn't blame him, I just didn't understand what was going on. I lost contact with that friend and have never been able to find him and let him know it wasn't his fault. I have done all I can to try to find him but his name is so common it is proven impossible for me to find him. If you ever meet a man named James Smith who served in Baumholder Germany with his wife Rose (from Brooklyn NY) please let them know I've never forgot the love and compassion they showed my wife and family while I was deployed!

These types of events continued on even though within just a few weeks after returning to Germany I PCS'd to Ft Sill Oklahoma for another eight months before leaving the Military. My new unit did a rotation to NTC where I was assigned as a driver for our section. During our training rotation we were overrun by OP-Four and the next thing I know the Captain was screaming at me in the driver's hatch of my vehicle a M577A2 Command Post Carrier almost five miles from our previous location. He then stopped suddenly in the middle of his butt chewing and instead he used a calm voice and asked; Sgt Kidman, are you alright? I turned my head toward him and never said a word, I just stared into his eyes and he into mine. I  experienced a flashback for the third time. Nothing was ever mentioned about that night after that even though my actions had caused a lot of equipment to be destroyed. The Captain realized as he could see in my eyes that I wasn't in NTC during that drive, but I was back in Iraq.

My next flashback is the one I regret the most and when I realized I really had a problem. It also erupted on a Sunday just after arriving home from morning church services. My wife was preparing lunch while I decided to take an eyelid inspection on the couch. Our son was only a little over three years old, when he came running into the living room to wake up Daddy for lunch. In his innocence he hit me at a full gallop right in the chest. By the time I actually was awake enough to know what I was doing I had already knocked him across the room into a wall just from reflexes. My heart sunk as I tried to comfort him but I could see the fear in his eyes. I was still in the Army at Fort Sill, OK and angry because no one ever warned us about things like this happening. I became ever angrier and it took less and less to invoke my rage.

My next experience happened at a family get together later that summer after getting out of the military. We all met at a campground in northern 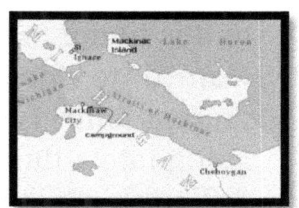 Michigan for a weekend of family, games and fun. The campground was on the shore of Lake Huron with a view of both sides of the Straights of Mackinaw and also Mackinaw Island, and the city of Cheboygan. The biggest reason we chose this destination was because it was the Fourth of July weekend and from that shoreline you could see the fireworks from each of those places. We found a great spot out on the shore and cooked over a fire as we awaited night fall and the wonderful fireworks I had always enjoyed as a kid, not knowing that this time it was going to be different. This time as the rockets' red glare and bombs bursting in air started I began to weep uncontrollably and my body began to tremble so I ran and hid from the rest of my family. Several times I tried to enjoy fireworks once again the result would be the same, because they did not mean the same thing to me anymore. Through the years I have learned to avoid fireworks as they are what we call a trigger into the past. From time to time I have been invited to an event or place such as a Ball game or water park unknowing that they were going to have fireworks that evening and the sights, sounds and smell put me into what I call the other world. As stated before when triggered my mind leaves this world and goes into the past world of the war. I refer

47

to this living in two worlds. When this happens I have learned to focus on something I know is in this present time (world) and that helps keep me from going into a flashback (the other world), but it is still a difficult time that overwhelms me in rage and puts me on high alert for hours or even days at times.

Finally one of the things that affected me greatly was the relationship I had with my children and especially our daughter who was born just prior to my deployment to Desert Storm. There were the many training exercises and then my units deployment, so I was gone her entire first year. This affected her perception of me, because I never had the opportunity to build that most important relationship during her first year of being a father and daughter. When I came home from the war she had no idea who I was and would scream at the top of her lungs every time I touched her mother or brother. Again my past or in this case the lack of it caused problems in the life of my family as well as for me personally.

These are not the only events that occurred in our lives but I chose these four because each one is different and we all must understand that there is no "one" response to combat, as there is no one response to our past.

It has been over thirty years since my unit came home from our combat mission in Desert Shield and Desert Storm. In those thirty years I have faced and battled what one can only describe as a monster within; that disrupts my sleep, makes me jump at unknown noises, makes me distant and irritable and at times comes out in a rage of anger. It took decades for me to understand what was really going on when this would happen and nearly another decade to get the words to describe PTSD in terms that everyone can easily understand.

DEPRESSION

Over twenty-eight years later my wife and I were nearly in what would have been a horrific accident. There was no accident but in my mind I saw it happen and that beast called PTSD ragged into depression and anxiety like I never knew existed. We were traveling down I-35 in WV when just around the corner the traffic was completely stopped in our lane with two cars and a semi coming towards us. There wasn't enough room to stop but by God's Grace alone we stopped just short of the vehicle in front of us. It was such a close call that my eyes were blurry and I could hardly see. My arms were numb and tingling with needles as I gasped for breath and trying not to pass out. After the traffic in front of me finally moved I couldn't get my foot off the brake and just set there for over fifteen minutes. This event launched me into a side of PTSD I had never know before.

I used to love to drive but now I didn't enjoy it and would get stressed every time we had to move our RV that we lived full-time in. I couldn't go out in public without being startled out of my skin over the littlest of things. When driving if something blew across the road in front of me I saw a grenade when it was nothing more than a soda can. At a restaurant someone would drop a dish and I would collapse in shock taking hours for my wife to get me back into this world. We would go to church and there would be a squelch on the PA system that would send me into a low-crawl out the door to safety. I got to the point that I didn't want to be around anyone except family and then only a few at a time.

I got to the point that I didn't even want to travel any more as we had for the past twelve years. I could go to a "shooting range" as long as I knew everyone that was there and knew when they were shooting but if a car backfired or weapons were fired near me that I didn't know were happening I would go into a rage of anger ready to fight to the death. At times things got so bad that I would contemplate just putting an end to it all. I was tired and constantly irritable, there was no joy in my life even though I was a Born Again Christian I begged God for help, yet felt like I had been abandoned by Him. Fear, stress, distrust, and anger became my life. In the middle of all this I had a total knee replacement and the drugs they put me on for pain didn't help my mental state at all. I was confused, angry, in tremendous pain and constantly in a state of high alert because of my PTSD.

HYPOCRISY

I had spent the past fourteen years traveling across America helping other Veterans learn to trust the LORD and that he would supply them with a Peace that passes all understanding but during this highlighted experience with PTSD I had very little peace within my own soul as I continued to try to help others see their need for God. I felt so hypocritical in my own heart yet knew that what I believed and taught to others was the only thing that could or would bring me out of this terrible experience. I tried to hide my pain but it would show through especially to my wife and occasionally I would just collapse in grief. This happened several times in meetings and those around me had no idea what or why I was falling apart. They would pray for me and although that was a comfort to my heart it seemed at times to be more of a comfort for them to ease their conscious because they didn't know what to do for me.

I knew the TRUTH of God's word but couldn't figure out why God wasn't answering my prayers for help and if he wouldn't help me then how could I tell others to trust Him to help them.

ANXIETY

I was never known for being an anxious person but all this turned me into someone who was always anxious about everything. I became paranoid of accidents, if a vehicle approached an intersection too fast I just knew they were going to drive through and hit me. If walking through a store I saw the same person twice, I was convinced we were being followed. I felt like everyone was judging me because of the hypocrisies I saw in my own life and before long they would tell everyone else about my failures. Trust had gone out the window and I was suspicious of anyone that wanted to become or remain my friend. It seemed that everything about me was failing one after another and God was nowhere to be found.

1 Corinthians 3:12-15 *Now if any man build upon this foundation gold, silver, precious stones, wood, hay, stubble; (13) Every man's work shall be made manifest: for the day shall declare it, because it shall be revealed by fire; and the fire shall try every man's work of what sort it is. (14) If any man's work abide which he hath built thereupon, he shall receive a reward. (15) If any man's work shall be burned, he shall suffer loss: but he himself shall be saved; yet so as by fire.*

TRIED BY FIRE

I didn't know it at the time but I was being tried by fire! All these issues added a level of stress to my life caused me to really figure out what I believed and why I believed. What has made many men quit and leave the ministry, although painful, in the end has made me stronger and a better soldier for the Lord! What the devil meant for evil, God has most definitely used for good! It was during those darkest hours that I began receiving phone calls and letters of how our ministry had helped other Veterans. In the years we have served in this ministry five Veterans have let us know that the day we met them they intended to commit suicide, but through us God spared them. One Veteran told me that although five have told us that, there are many more that we will not know about until God personally reveals them to us in Glory!

D—PLANNED DISORDER

The last word in PTSD is disorder which many take as the thought that because we have PTSD we are broken or disturbed and in disorder. The problem is that for most it is because they are looking from the outside in without a context of what they are seeing. Like a good map needs a legend, so to do many need a key or legend to understand how PTSD affects us. At times it feels as if the whole world is against us because they don't understand what we are going through. This misunderstanding translates into mistrust, fear and anxiety of anyone labeled as having PTSD. As my Dad had told me before we deployed as Veterans we have become the whore of the nation.

ARE YOU A VETERAN?

For the first several years after getting out of the military when I would fill out an application for a job there was always that one question: Are you a Veteran? Then which branch and the date you joined and when you ETS (End Time in Service). At first I was proud to be able to answer those questions by providing the requested information, but as time wore on I began to realize that by answering those questions I was giving that perspective employer a reason not to hire me. Even when I would get as far as an interview, the questions would come up again so I would begin to list my qualifications based upon my leadership training and experience in the military. They would ask what did you actually do in the military and I would proudly say Field Artillery and chemical warfare. They would look me in the eye and say something like well we really don't need anything or anyone blown up so that really doesn't apply to the position we have available and dismiss me as a candidate for that position.

Never did anyone take into consideration what qualities were required in a leader to get men to follow him into battle where the outcome was uncertain. They did not take into consideration the fact that we had to become proficient at training others, no matter the subject we trained those under our command to perform their tasks effectively and also to learn the tasks of every person in the section. All perspective employers saw was a man of war who taught war, lived war and breathed war. They never took my military leadership skills seriously regardless of how well I presented it because they were afraid of the "disorder" that was associated with war and PTSD. THEIR LOSS! I eventually got to the point where I wouldn't put on an application that I was a combat Veteran or even just a Veteran, I'd leave that question blank because of the stigma that was associated with the question.

DISORDER LEARNED IN BASIC

However, the real aspect of the disorder associated with PTSD is not what happens now, it is what was put within us during our training. An Airborne Ranger once handed me a book called "On Killing" it was a psychological look at what it takes for one man to kill another in combat. This included police officers who had to engage in armed conflict during an arrest situation. The author did a lot of research on this subject looking back at the many wars we have fought in including the American Revolutionary War. Throughout his study he had found that prior to the Vietnam War it was typical that less than 25% of soldiers in a battle would continue the fight once the first volley had been fired. Although a "Picket Line" would shoot at 85% accuracy at targets, that same "Picket Line" in combat would lose over 75% of their personal who would find other things to do rather than fight. Some carried the dead and wounded, others went for more ammo, while yet others would just stop fighting altogether.

During Vietnam the military changed its training practices and the result was now over 85% of soldiers would stay in the fight during a battle. In post Vietnam era that percentage was increased even more resulting in a military that would not just go to war but one in which the members were ready to fight to the last ounce of strength. Often times throughout this book I have spoken about the "rage" from battle and I can trace that rage back to the training we received during basic training. We were taught to fight hand to hand and the whole group punished if any one of us gave up and did not give our all to the battle. I can remember the Drill Instructors yelling at us "get angry, do whatever it takes to win" and other phrases like that as we were fighting each other in the sand pits. When a soldier would get tired and start to lose in battle the Drill Instructors would shout anything they could think of about what our enemy would do to our loved ones to motivate us to fight a little longer and harder. When that rage kicked in it was an adrenaline rush of power, energy and strength, like a second wind. This training and disorder continued to be reinforced in everything we did in basic becoming a "muscle memory".

DISORDER REINFORCED

The disorder continued to be reinforced when I reached my first unit. We were told not to fraternize with the upper enlisted or offices, yet as a young private I was playing racquetball every Thursday with my 1st Sgt, XO (Executive Officer) and my Battalion CSM. I was assigned as the driver for our Gunnery Sgt and advanced party, but also had to drive for the Platoon Sgt and still find time to learn more about my MOS. At one point I found myself as just a Private First Class (PFC) in charge of my FDC section for an entire week while we were out in the field training. My section chief (E6) was having an operation and the Corporal (E4P) who was second in command became deathly ill and had to be medevaced to the hospital. This left me and two other privates to shoot, move and communicate for 1st Platoon FDC 1st BN 3rd FA. At the end of the week my FDO Lieutenant was so impressed that he put me in for an award. I still did my job as driver for Gunnery Sgt, my own advance party and then set up and operated the FDC doing the job of not one but two ranks above my pay grade. Ok, yes even I was impressed with myself at that point, but it taught me to persevere when the unexpected comes because there are usually others counting on you. When the observer called on the radio for a Fire Mission, he did not know he was talking to a private. When the mission data was sent to the cannons, those E6 Gun Chiefs had no idea that it was just a private giving them the order to fire. Others were counting on someone to be there when they needed our unit to fire and that fell upon me. Then I also had the care of the two younger and lower rank soldiers in my section. I had to make sure they were fed, got rest, drank enough water ...etc. It was a huge responsibility for someone who had only been in the Army for a few months.

DISORDER IN TRAINING

After having proved myself, I was quickly promoted to specialist at 11 months in service and sent to the E5 Sgt Board at 15 months in service. I was no longer on advance party and had been replaced as the Gunnery Sgt's driver too. I was now the second in command of my section and the primary computer operator for FDC operations. That summer my FDO, Staff Sgt (Section Chief) and I were sent out to evaluate other artillery units. Several times in my short career my unit had been evaluated and now it was me in that position of examining others who did my same job. One unit we were sent too was where I had my second biggest challenge to this point. They were an Army

Reserve Unit and had an E7 as their section Chief which is usually an E6 position. It is the Section Chief and FDO's responsibility to make sure they are firing data that is "SAFE". In other words when the rounds go down range we needed to make sure they were a "SAFE" distance from friendly troops. In my position as primary computer operator it was also something that I had to learn how to do and now I had to evaluate others on this and other tasks in the process of firing artillery.

When I looked at their computations for Safety it was all wrong and it would be easy for them to fire "OUT OF SAFE" endangering friendly troops. Immediately I shut them down from firing any live ammunition until they resolved their safety issues. This did not go over well, that an E4 was telling an E7 Sgt and his FDO Lieutenant that their safety computations were wrong. That was just the start of it, as their Captain rolled in demanding to know what was going on so I briefed him of the situation. The next thing I know a Full Bird Colonel, a two star General and their three star General all in their command showed up and my rear end was in the hot seat. Each one as they arrive and were briefed of the situation confronted me demanding that I allow that unit to shoot live missions so they could qualify as battle ready. Each time I had to look that officer in the eye as just an E4 and tell them NO SIR!

The problem was that none of them had ever learned how to properly compute safety data so no one there was qualified to bring them back to a live fire status. When the Lieutenant General (3 stars) faced off with me and began chewing me out my FDO stepped in and backed me up. He took the chewing for me, but more importantly he had my six as we say. I gained a lot of respect for him that day, which was hard earned when it came to officers. Finally while my Section Chief and FDO went home for the evening, I stayed there and taught them how to do "Safety". I wasn't supposed to do that kind of thing, but I looked at it this way, one day we may have to depend upon this unit to help us out of a battle and I want them doing things right. My Section Chief and FDO agreed. The following morning when the range opened we were able to give them the green light to fire live missions and they passed their evaluation with flying colors.

That was my first experience where my position gave me power over others who obviously out ranked me. That seemed like a huge disorder to all who were involved, including myself, but it was all proper according to military protocol. My rank meant nothing, but my position as part of the evaluation team meant everything. What started out as disorder become proper training in an otherwise improper way. E7's teach E4's not the other way around… HOOAH!

DISORDER IN COMBAT

Earlier in this book I explained how I was moved into a section during combat where the section chief did not know his job and had proved it over and over. What I did not mention before was that I was transferred there at my Captains request to make sure that FDC functioned properly during combat. This did cause a little bit of disorder as I was still only an E5 Sgt and the actual Chief was an E6. The Captain had tried to get some other E6's from other units to transfer here to take his place but that never worked out so the lot fell upon my shoulders.

Things went somewhat smoothly at first while we were preparing our vehicles for battle after they were unloaded off the ship in Saudi Arabia in the port of Duran. When we finally left there and moved within 100 miles of the Iraqi border that's when things started to heat up a bit. I had been tasked with driving another vehicle out to the forward deployment area so I wasn't with the section until later that evening. When I arrived the section chief had thrown out a lot of equipment into a big hole he had the privates dig, including all the cots. I grabbed a cot and said "I'm not sleeping on the ground if I can help it." When I questioned him about why he was tossing all our equipment he became irate and began a huge argument between the two of us. He was signed for all that equipment so I really didn't care about most of it. However, during that argument I had to establish myself as to why I was there as his second in command.

I asserted myself that even though he was signed for the vehicle and all its equipment, from now on they were mine and he was not to touch them. He had a reputation for breaking anything he touched and that was the primary reason I was sent to his section. Secondly I informed him that although he is the "Chief" of the section the soldiers under our command were mine as well. Anything he had to say to them was to go through me first. I relieved him of the responsibility of caring for their welfare. I also assumed the responsibility of scheduling their daily duties. I did give him permission to engage with any officer who entered our vehicle to keep them out of my hair. Needless to say all this did not go over well with him as we continued to yell at each other. Finally he asked me on what authority was I taking position over him even though I was a lower rank. I had had enough and simply said "The Captain placed me here with full authority to take over this section and if you don't like it take it up with him".

Throughout our tour of duty he made my life a living hell as he would make accusations against me that kept me from going to the next E6 board even though I had been promised that would still happen after I changed sections. He wrote me up for being overweight, even though we had no way of being weighed so I couldn't prove he was making these things up. He deliberately assigned me a radio watch time during the same time I was supposed to be the Sgt of the Guard for the night so I would have conflicting orders so either way I was going to disobey one or the other and he could bring me up on charges of disobeying orders and being AWOL from my appointed duties. He was constantly a thorn in my side throughout the rest of our deployment, but he didn't get away with his game as the Captain made sure those charges were dropped and upon returning home to Baumholder Germany offered me an opportunity to go to the E6 board. I thanked him and said I would love to do that if my old section chief was the one who took me to the board instead of the one I had just fought a war with during the Persian Gulf War. I was not allowed to do that so I declined. Later I regretted that decision but in the end it all turned out fine.

Throughout this book I have shared many things that I have faced because of PTSD issues both during my service and afterwards. The purpose is not to show what a terrible time I had in the military or afterwards, but to show that even though I went through some terrible things, I was able to persevere. In the last chapter I will explain how I was able to persevere through many tough and dark days because of my PTSD.

DISORDERLY NORMAL

It was just after the first battle we fought in that you could hear some men laughing and joking, others were angry and pounding inanimate objects, some were just sitting in the corner in a blank stare or talking to themselves. My Lieutenant placed his hand on my shoulder and said "there is no normal reaction to war". Usually I didn't like officers much but his words at that particular time made a lot of sense to me. Each one's response to battle was different and each battle would generate a different response for any individual. One time they would laugh and the next time they were in tears. One time they were silent and the next time they were the host of the party talking loudly. What is my point, THERE IS NO NORMAL, JUST DIFFERENT!

PTSD has had many names throughout history when my Dad served in WWII it was called "Shell Shock" at other times it has been called "Battle Fatigue" or "The Thousand Mile Stare". It's not the name but the effect of what we have experienced that remains the same. Everyone who has experienced War has come home different than they left.

PLANNED DISORDER

The disorder in PTSD is not as much a result of what happened to us in war as it is about what happened to us in training. In basic training we were broke down, physically, mentally and spiritually. The physical aspect is what most people associate with basic but the main emphasis was on the mental and spiritual aspects of warfare. Whether physical, mental or spiritual we had to learn endurance when everything seems to be falling apart. Physically we had to learn our strengths and then be pushed far beyond what we thought ourselves capable of. Mentally we had to learn that barriers that we had placed upon ourselves could be broken when we placed our mind to believe it could. Spiritually we were challenged the most, because it is hard for some to see Jehovah God in War. When he no longer fits the peace, love and joy teachings from Sunday School or VBS we question if HE is really real or not. However, like my platoon Sgt only knew "thou shalt not kill" many have never come to realize that although Jehovah God is Love, and Peace and Joy, He is also a jealous God of wrath and judgment. Because He is righteous He must judge all sin. Often times in the scriptures we find that God used one nation to judge another nation in an act of WAR.

All this leads to the fact that the disorder started long before we ever deployed to a war zone. This kind of disorder is not natural it has to be taught and trained upon over and over to make it become what feels like a natural reaction. "Muscle memory", much needed in combat, but totally misunderstood in civilian life. PTSD doesn't make us a weaker person unless we let it. It is not a sign of weakness or instability; it is rather a sign of strength and stability that is needed when facing the enemy in armed combat.

The greatest chapter in this book is next as we read about a shepherd by the name of David who became King of Israel. Before he became King he was a faithful servant and accomplished warrior. However he had his turn at the wheel of what we now call PTSD and learning how King David dealt with it has been a huge blessing and encouragement to my life.

It doesn't matter what your "religious" views are, you won't want to skip over chapter five. It is the summary of all we have discussed so far. It can only help, but only if you will let it!

KING DAVID ON PTSD

So what does King David have to do with PTSD? Well, first of all whether or not you believe in God or the Bible there are volumes of documentation on the existence of a man named David that became the King of Israel. Secondly throughout my career in the military the subject of my faith in God would come up between those I worked with. From the Corporal who ordered me not to talk about God, to the Gunnery Sgt I drove for and various Lieutenants amongst others in my command upon occasion. However, it was the time spent talking with several lieutenants and other officers that I learned that the life of King David was required reading for officers at that time. I was intrigued to learn that and would ask each officer I worked with, why they thought that was, and what they learned from their study of King David?

One of the first things an officer told me he learned was actually my first point that there is much historical evidence to the life and times of the King David of the Bible. This lieutenant wasn't really a "religious" man but after studying about David through historical documents and the Bible he was searching and he was interested in the acts of "Faith" that David was known for. Most people are at least familiar with the story of David and Goliath and the battle fought by these two men. Yet at the time of that battle David was only a teenager, the youngest of his siblings assigned as to be the shepherd of his father's flock of sheep. The only reason David was even at the battle field that day was because his father asked him to take supplies to his older brothers who were in the army of Israel.

OBEDIENCE

David became a great king because he was dedicated to being obedient to his Father's will.

1Samuael 17:17-18 *And Jesse said unto David his son, Take now for thy brethren an ephah of this parched corn, and these ten loaves, and run to the camp to thy brethren; (18) And carry these ten cheeses unto the captain of their thousand, and look how thy brethren fare, and take their pledge.*

While David was in the camp Goliath made his daily challenge for just one man of Israel to fight him alone and the winner would decide the outcome of the battle. What shocked David was that none of the men of Israel were willing to respond to this challenge. Maybe it was because Goliath had been a man of war since his youth and was a well seasoned warrior. Maybe it is because all historical information about this battle lists Goliath as a "Giant" because the average height of a man of Israel was between 5-6ft tall and Goliath was over 9ft tall. Regardless of the many other reasons that could be listed here, no one was willing to answer this man's challenge.

This is where David comes in as just a rutty youth and answers the call to battle with this, his battle cry "is there not a cause?" when questioned by Israel's King at that time as to his qualifications David responds with a most unique answer.

1Samuael 17:34-36 *And David said unto Saul, Thy servant kept his father's sheep, and there came a lion, and a bear, and took a lamb out of the flock: (35) And I went out after him, and smote him, and delivered it out of his mouth: and when he arose against me, I caught him by his beard, and smote him, and slew him. (36) Thy servant slew both the lion and the bear: and this uncircumcised Philistine shall be as one of them, seeing he hath defied the armies of the living God.*

Can you imagine grabbing a lion by the beard? Not me there are teeth on that end. Mind you, a sling, staff and possibly a small dagger were all David had to fight with. These were not the usual weapons of war that one would rush into battle against a bear or lion, let alone a 9ft tall giant. The men of Israel were living in fear of a giant, like most people today are living in fear of big government, disease and an unstable world all around them. Add PTSD to that mixture and it's not hard to understand why so many Veterans fall into depression.

LOYALTY

The second reason for studying King David was how he fully relied on God throughout his life as a shepherd, solider and King. After the battle with Goliath, King Saul took an interest in the youth named David. Saul kept David close to him as David rose up through the ranks of the military. He advanced himself through victory in battle and became a fierce warrior. So much so that King Saul became jealous of him when all Israel began to praise David more than they did their King.

1Samuael 18:6-8 *And it came to pass as they came, when David was returned from the slaughter of the Philistine, that the women came out of all cities of Israel, singing and dancing, to meet king Saul, with tabrets, with joy, and with instruments of musick. (7) And the women answered one another as they played, and said, Saul hath slain his thousands, and David his ten thousands. (8) And Saul was very wroth, and the saying displeased him; and he said, They have ascribed unto David ten thousands, and to me they have ascribed but thousands: and what can he have more but the kingdom?*

The boy who had become aid to the King and a mighty warrior for the armies of Israel was now in peril from the one man he was loyal to protect and serve as Saul began jealously seek to kill David.

1Samuael 18:9-12 *And Saul eyed David from that day and forward. (10) And it came to pass on the morrow, that the evil spirit from God came upon Saul, and he prophesied in the midst of the house: and David played with his hand, as at other times: and there was a javelin in Saul's hand. (11) And Saul cast the javelin; for he said, I will smite David even to the wall with it. And David avoided out of his presence twice. (12) And Saul was afraid of David, because the LORD was with him, and was departed from Saul.*

As near as I have been able to count King Saul made 21 attempts on David's life, while David stayed loyal regardless.

DEDICATED

Like David many of us have fought the enemy only to return to a nation and dare I say a political system that now considers us a threat because of what that same government taught us to do in battle. There are many things we could discuss or even argue about in our government, but it is the government that the Lord has given us. I therefore will stay loyal to the country that I fought for and the principles upon which it was founded. I will stay faithful to the Constitution which is the LAW that binds us as a people. Personally I, like King David, choose to follow the teachings of the Word of God:

Romans 12:9-21 *Let love be without dissimulation. Abhor that which is evil; cleave to that which is good. (10) Be kindly affectioned one to another with brotherly love; in honour preferring one another; (11) Not slothful in business; fervent in spirit; serving the Lord; (12) Rejoicing in hope; patient in tribulation; continuing instant in prayer; (13) Distributing to the necessity of saints; given to hospitality. (14) Bless them which persecute you: bless, and curse not. (15) Rejoice with them that do rejoice, and weep with them that weep. (16) Be of the same mind one toward another. Mind not high things,* *but condescend to men of low estate. Be not wise in your own conceits. (17) Recompense to no man evil for evil. <u>Provide things honest in the sight of all men. (18) If it be possible, as much as lieth in you, live peaceably with all men.</u> (19) Dearly beloved, avenge not yourselves, but rather give place unto wrath: for it is written, Vengeance is mine; I will repay, saith the Lord. (20) Therefore if thine enemy hunger, feed him; if he thirst, give him drink: for in so doing thou shalt heap coals of fire on his head. (21) <u>Be not overcome ofevil, but overcome evil with good.</u>*

Don't get me wrong, I am no sheep but a well trained sheepdog ever on vigilant watch against those who would perpetrate evil upon innocent people. Even so, I believe and practice what is taught in the above scriptures and have found that verse 21 is better than the sword!

TEMPTATION AND TROUBLES

Once David became King his battles were not over, actually some of his most difficult battles lie ahead of him. One of his most difficult battles was his flesh when he was tempted into the sin of adultery. He was the King and should have been leading his army into war; instead he stayed home and sent his troops to battle. Although he was King he was in the wrong place at the right time and fell into lust over a young married woman. She was the bride of one of David's chief warriors. The sin from this battle cost him peace in his home as his children began to turn away from the God he served. Even though David repented of his sin and got things right with God, he still suffered the consequences of that sin. One of his sons raped his own sister, another son killed that son, and yet another son overthrew his Kingdom ousting his very own father from the thrown. His life was riddled with disappointment and regrets, yet though this entire time he kept his focus on serving the God of his Fathers the Lord God JEHOVAH.

COURAGE

In battle after battle, year after year, even as a King he was a courageous leader. People are looking for courageous leaders who will stand when everyone else folds. It has been said that everything rises and falls upon leadership. The problems in David's family are a result of poor leadership in his home. On the other hand his years in battle made him the perfect leader in times of war. Let us be perfectly clear that courage is not the lack of fear, but the ability to function in the face of fear instead of being controlled by it. David said this...

Psalm 27:11-14 *Teach me thy way, O LORD, and lead me in a plain path, because of mine enemies. (12) Deliver me not over unto the will of mine enemies: for false witnesses are risen up against me, and such as breathe out cruelty. (13) I had fainted, unless I had believed to see the goodness of the LORD in the land of the living. (14)* <u>*Wait on the LORD:* **be of good courage,** *and he shall strengthen thine heart: wait, I say, on the LORD*</u>.

In the New Testament God gave this testimony about King David:

Act 13:21-22 *And afterward they desired a king: and God gave unto them Saul the son of Cis, a man of the tribe of Benjamin, by the space of forty years. (22) And when he had removed him, he raised up unto them David to be their king; to whom also he gave testimony, and said, I have found David the son of Jesse, a man after mine own heart, which shall fulfil all my will.*

Even though David was not a perfect man he kept a perfect heart before the Lord. Whenever he sinned he made sure he kept a short account with God by repenting to keep his heart after the Lord. Let me just clarify one thing, being a soldier in war is not a sin, it is God using one nation to judge another nation through the act of war. However, of the tens of thousands of those King David killed in battle he sinned against the Lord when he committed adultery with Bathsheba and then had her husband killed in battle. That was murder and one of the many times David had to repent. It was also the one thing that kept him from building the Temple for the Lord because of the blood on his hands.

KING DAVID ON PTSD

In 2020 I was preparing to preach over Veterans Day weekend in a church that had a lot of Combat Veterans and actually that day they had even more come in for the services. I knew that church had a couple of WWII guys, several which served during the Korean and Vietnam wars, as well some from Iraq and Afghanistan. I had been praying for the Lords leadership and the thought came to me about PTSD in the Bible. However preaching is far more than just a thought, it has to have a foundation found and built upon scriptural context and truth. I had just been reading through the Bible and as it so happened my reading that day fell upon the 23rd Psalm. I had used this scripture many times for funerals but as I looked at it that day I saw that it wasn't a Psalm of death but a Psalm of "LIFE"!

The book of Psalms is one of the most profound books of the Bible. When we consider that of all the Psalms in the Bible King David wrote the majority of them. Of the ones King David wrote, most of them are as he was entering into war, during war, or just after the victory. David lived a life of a warrior that desired peace and as King he made sure his people had peace by never being afraid of war. The 23rd Psalm is no exception to this and in fact is the very essence of David's desire for peace. I would not be offended if you the reader disagreed with me on this, because it will not change my heart or mind. Personally I believe that the 23rd Psalm is King David's manifesto on his struggle with what we call PTSD today! I have learned when PTSD strikes to quote this powerful Psalm and have found it gives me peace.

David wrote in Psalm 18:34 *He teacheth my hands to*

war, so that a bow of steel is broken by mine arms.

Again David wrote in Psalm 144:1 A Psalm of David. *Blessed be the LORD my strength, which teacheth my hands to war, and my fingers to fight:*

These are just two examples where King David gives Honor and Glory to God because David knew and understood that God created him a warrior and a King. Yet it is in the 23rd Psalm that because of all the fighting King David did he yearned for peace. He found that peace in the Lord God Jehovah, in His word and precepts. Herein are David's thoughts as well as other Scriptures to support King David's message.

The 23rd Psalm only has six verses and I have broken these six verses down into three segments. Each segment will be alliterated by the initials PTSD. So with no more a due, let's take a look at this Psalm of David, King of Israel, a Man of War!

King James Bible

(1)   **A Psalm of David.** The LORD *is* my shepherd; I shall not want.

P.   He is my Provider, David learned early on in life that God knows our every need and therefore we can trust that whatever happens in our lives He will, is and can supply as our provider. Matthew_6:8 *Be not ye therefore like unto them: for your Father knoweth what things ye have need of, before ye ask him.*

T.   He is my Teacher, ever learning to trust where he

leads me as the Good Shepherd. Psalm 86:11 *Teach me thy way, O LORD; I will walk in thy truth: unite my heart to fear thy name.*

(2) He maketh me to lie down in green pastures: he leadeth me beside the still waters.

S. He is my Supply: As my provider. He makes sure we have the supplies we need like food and water and so much more. As my Supply He is the very food and water we need. Philippians 4:19 *But my God shall supply all your need according to his riches in glory by Christ Jesus.*

(3) He restoreth my soul: he leadeth me in the paths of righteousness for his name's sake.

D. He is my Restoration Galatians 6:1 *Brethren, if a man be overtaken in a fault, ye which are spiritual, restore such an one in the spirit of meekness; considering thyself, lest thou also be tempted.*

He is my Determination, Proverbs 21:3 *To do justice and judgment is more acceptable to the LORD than sacrifice.*

(4) Yea, though I walk through the valley of the shadow of death, I will fear no evil: for thou *art* with me; thy rod and thy staff they comfort me.

P. He is my Protection in the face of death. Often David refers to God as his Shield. Psalms 18:35 *Thou hast also given me the shield of thy salvation: and thy right hand hath holden me up, and thy gentleness hath made me great.*

T.   He is my Treasure, because he is always with us. Romans 8:31 W*hat shall we then say to these things? If God be for us, who can be against us*?

S.   He is my Saviour; David looked for the coming Messiah and put his faith in Jesus Christ for his salvation. Psalm 18:2b ...*my buckler, and the horn of my salvation, and my high tower*.

D.   He is my Deliverer, David knew that only the Messiah would be able to deliver him physically and spiritually. Psalm 18:2a *The LORD is my rock, and my fortress, and my deliverer; my God, my strength, in whom I will trust*;

(5a)   Thou preparest a table before me in the presence of mine enemies:

P.   He is my Promise, God's promises are for everlasting 2Peter 1:4 *Whereby are given unto us exceeding great and precious promises: that by these ye might be partakers of the divine nature, having escaped the corruption that is in the world through lust.*

(5b)   ...thou anointest my head with oil; my cup runneth over.

T.   He is my Trust, the source of all that I trust. Proverbs 3:1-6 *My son, forget not my law; but let thine heart keep my commandments: (2) For length of days, and long life, and peace, shall they add to thee. (3) Let not mercy and truth forsake thee: bind them about thy neck; write them upon the table of thine heart: (4) So shalt thou find favour and good understanding in the sight of God and man. (5) <u>Trust in the LORD with all</u>*

thine heart; and lean not unto thine own understanding. *(6) In all thy ways acknowledge him, and he shall direct thy paths.*

(6a)   Surely goodness and mercy shall follow me all the days of my life:

S.   He is my Serenity, the state of being calm, peaceful, and untroubled Psalms 27:13 *I had fainted, unless I had believed to see the goodness of the LORD in the land of the living.*

(6b)   … and I will dwell in the house of the LORD for ever.

D.   He is my Delight and the hope of my eternal destination. John 14:1-3 *Let not your heart be troubled: ye believe in God, believe also in me. (2) In my Father's house are many mansions: if it were not so, I would have told you. I go to prepare a place for you. (3) And if I go and prepare a place for you, I will come again, and receive you unto myself; that where I am, there ye may be also.*

Shortly after preaching this message I was scrolling through one of my social media accounts and found an Iraqi War Veteran's video with the title "PTSD IN THE BIBLE". I thought to myself, no way, so I had to listen to it all the way through. As it began I wondered who was this Veteran, what church he attended if any, what was his motive for this particular video and many more questions went through my mind. I listened to his message as it really spoke to my heart how this man whom I had never met before, in another State hundreds of miles away, with a ministry to Veterans similar to ours, out of a Baptist Church I had never heard of, preached my outline thought for thought, nearly word for word using a King James Bible.

I was overwhelmed to think how God had given that message to me and there is no way this guy could have ever heard it so soon after I preached it. I had to contact him and find out more about this man. I messaged him my information and asked him to call me at his earliest convenience. When he called me I began pumping him for information on why he preached this message and where he got the idea from and why was it so important to him. He answered a few questions and then stopped me from asking anymore and now had a question for me. "Why do you want to know?" he asked.

I backed up and began telling him about the Ministry to Veterans God had put us in nearly 14 years ago at that time. Then explained that his message was the same one I had just preached on Veterans Day in NC and he was in MO. We discussed what lead us to each point of the message and became good ol' friends in a very short time, all in one day. You see it didn't bother me that someone else had the same message, even if it had been because he heard me preach it through the internet somehow. On the contrary, it excited me to know God gave the same message to two individual's miles apart that did not know the other existed, and He did it at the same time! That my friend was the Lord God Jehovah letting both know; it was of Him and not of us.

Since that time we have become good friends and had

at least one opportunity to meet each other face to face. It is great to see that the Lord has shared our burden for the Military to know the Lord, with other Veterans too. We know many Military missionaries that are stationed near a particular military base and they are needed reaching those on active duty. But my friend this book has been handed to you so you too can know that there is a God in heaven that Loves you and sent His very own Son Jesus Christ to die for your sin. Being a warrior is not a sin, but we are all sinners in need of a Saviour.

He has sent us to reach as many with the good news that Jesus paid the debt of sin we could never pay. Jesus did not come to condemn us he came to liberate us from the bondage of sin and condemnation put upon us when the devil beguiled Eve in the Garden of Eden. God did not put us in a place of judgment Satan did. God has offered us a way to escape that judgment during this lifetime, but once that is over He MUST be a Righteous Judge of all humanity and carry out the sentencing process based upon the plea that was entered on our behalf. The prosecutor is the devil and he has entered his evidences of our sin as proof of why God must damn us to hell. However, Jesus has been provided as an advocate on our behalf, if we will but admit our guilt to him and put our faith and trust in Him and the Sacrifice for sin He made upon Mt Calvary. His services as an advocate are free to us but they cost Him His very life on the cross. As a man His sinless body died to become the acceptable offering made to God on our behalf. As God He ascended into hell paying our debt and on the third day as prophesied He arose from that same tomb in the same human body of man and conquered Death and Hell for you and me.

When you put your faith in Him you are accepting the work of Salvation He did for you and from that point forward you have an Advocate that stands up to the accuser Satan to show that He has already paid for all our transgressions.   Once you allow the Lord Jesus Christ to lift that burden from your shoulders you are truly "Born Again". This does not give us a license to sin, but just he contrary, it takes the desire to sin out of our hearts. There is no one that is perfect so as long as we are still in this "flesh" we will be tempted and it is up to us if and when we yield to those temptations. However, when we are tempted there is no joy in it anymore. We do not lose our Salvation but we lose fellowship with the Father. Our hearts desire at that point is to take it to the Lord in prayer in repentance to restore fellowship with God.

There is no magic prayer or words, but we must come to God with a contrite heart (broken).

The Bible teaches in Hebrews6:1 *Therefore leaving the principles of the doctrine of Christ, let us go on unto perfection; not laying again the foundation of* **repentance from dead works**, *and of* **faith toward God**,

What does **repentance from dead works** mean, it

simply means that we must repent, be sorrowful toward God for whatever religion, creed, belief, non-belief …etc…we trusted in that has kept us from trusting Jesus Christ.

What does **faith toward God** mean, it simply means to replace our previous system of belief with "Faith" that God is who He said he was and that Jesus Christ His Son is the one through whom God has given the only path of Salvation. John14:6 *Jesus saith unto him, I am the way, the truth, and the life: no man cometh unto the Father, but by me.*

King David found the peace that passes all understanding because he found and acted upon his need of a Saviour. Philippians 4:7 *And the peace of God, which passeth all understanding, shall keep your hearts and minds through Christ Jesus.*

David was still effected throughout his life by PTSD, but now he had a tool given to him by God to sustain him even during his darkest hours. Like David I too still have issues from PTSD, but I have learned how to use PTSD to help others who are struggling from its effects. For example the idea for this book was birthed in my mind in June of 2021. I have written chapter one over and over but it never seemed to be right. Several times each year I would make an attempt to write, but no, it wasn't happening.

However, in the months of October and November of 2023 we were in four Baptist Churches in five weeks and in each of these Churches their PA system decided to peak-out with a very loud squelch noise that would trigger my PTSD. Six times this happened in those five weeks and four Churches; each time their sound man or Pastor told me they never have problems like this. The last time it happened I was told that I hit the ground in a fetal position and covered my ears as if expecting an explosion. I did not know that I wasn't the only one it affected and in the midst of all that going on I had yelled "leave him alone, don't touch". A Vietnam Veteran rushed to help us by blowing air in our faces and identifying himself without making contact. His actions helped bring both of us back to a point where we knew where we were but were still dealing with the rage of battle that was overwhelming us right then.

The other man left the building until he had calmed down enough to reenter the services, but he remained in the foyer just in case it happened again. I stayed in my pew for the rest of the service even though many things were continuing to trigger me, but I stayed for a reason. The reason was to "Stay in the Fight"! After the service was over I just sat there once the majority of people had left the building I finally got up to leave. My knees were weak and my head pounding from the episode but with a little assistance from my grown children I was able to make it. The Pastor and sound man came to me with tears in their eyes, apologizing for what had happened, my only response was "did I hurt anyone?" No one expected me to be back that night and I really didn't know if I was up to it or not but I went back for a reason. The reason was to "Stay in the Fight"! Wednesday evening I was there, you guessed it to "Stay in the Fight"!

On Sunday mornings they have a short "Opener" message before the call to prayer and then off to Sunday School classes. That Sunday I just happened to have the "Opener" and did it on PTSD in the Bible. All week long I had been thinking about how to handle what had happened the week before. Do I talk about it, just let it be, what could I even say that would help non-Veterans understand what had happened. Then on Friday the thoughts manifested into what has become the chapter headings and subject matter of this book I had all but given up on getting done.

I believe all of this was the devil attacking me through the sounds of the airwaves all six times. Even today as I was typing this chapter I got a voice message on my phone so I paused to listen to it. It was digital traffic and that signal began to trigger me again today. But that was just a coincidence right?

What the devil meant for evil God meant for good. The writer's block was gone and I clearly had direction from the Lord enough that in what I have not been able to accomplish in nearly three years was completed in just a little over 48 hours.

One Korean War Veteran invested in my life so God could us me to invest in thousands of Veterans each year. My Comrade you are not alone, please feel free to contact me at any time, leave a message and I will get back with you as soon as possible. Even if I cannot get to where you are located God has given us contacts all across the country and in several European countries.

ABOUT THE AUTHOR

Dr. Russell Kidman and his wife Cathy Founders of Operation Liberty Missionaries To Our Military

Brother Kidman was deployed to Operation Desert Shield and Operation Desert Storm during the Liberation of Kuwait in 1990-1991. He was a sergeant serving as a Fire Direction NCO and secondary Chemical Specialist for Alpha Battery 2nd Battalion 29th Field Artillery Unit. He was deployed as General Support Reinforcement to 42nd Brigade and 3rd Armor Division.

Brother Kidman and his wife are now missionaries to our military with a firsthand understanding of what the soldier who is deployed and the family who is left behind are experiencing. Most people see the soldier coming home but fail to realize the struggles of returning home and readjusting to civilian life and family. This is where Brother Kidman applies his experience and knowledge of God's Word to help our soldiers and their families from a Biblical perspective.

GOD CALLED

These Are My Credentials

SALVATION - 8/2/1980

While visiting my Dad one year after I had a terrible motorcycle accident, under heavy conviction, I told him that I needed to be saved. Right then and right there he led me to the Lord. What a wonderful and merciful God to allow me to be saved.

CALLING - 2/28/1988

Just one year after I was saved I believe God placed His call upon my life but I did not respond until I was in the military in Baumholder, Germany attending Grace Baptist Church. During revival services I answered the call to preach the gospel of the Lord Jesus Christ. God gave me three years under Pastor Tim Clark's leadership as he grounded me in the Word of God.

YOUTH MINISTRY - 6/14/1992

Upon leaving the military, I was asked to be youth pastor at a Baptist Church in my wife's home town. Within just a few years God moved me into a full-time position in the Detroit area. For 13 years my wife and I served the Lord leading many young souls to Christ.

MISSIONARY/EVANGELIST - 7/2/2006

Who knows how long God has been planning this, but as for me it all started with a return trip back to Grace Baptist Church of Baumholder, Germany to provide special music for a men's retreat in May of 2006. I returned home with a greater burden for all those serving our country. God had opened my eyes to see a need in our Reserve and National Guard Units, their families and our Veterans. - Evangelism 11/3/2003

EDUCATION

Midwestern Baptist College ~ Pontiac, MI
~ Associates of Arts Biblical Studies

86

Liberty Baptist Bible College ~ Newaygo, MI
 ~ Bachelors of Arts Biblical Studies
Liberty Baptist Theological Seminary ~ Newaygo, MI
 ~Masters of Theology
 ~ Doctor of Theology
American Christian University ~ Gastonia, NC
 ~ Doctor of Philosophy

Contact Information:

Dr. Russell Kidman Ph.D.
www.OperationLibertyMinistry.org

Where can I get more copies of this book?

The Old Paths Publications, Inc

www.theoldpathspublications.com
TOP@theoldpathspublications.com

Michael and many others to accompany Father Robin to the Pecos monastery in New Mexico U.S.A. to attend the well-known course there on Spiritual Direction. Since I had been at home all the time with Ken and he became better I had been called more and more to listen to people with inner problems and pray with them. They would come to the house; I had a room upstairs set aside for this which doubled as the prayer room for the prayer group after Ken had moved upstairs from the dining room. People came mostly from churches other than the Catholic Church for inner healing, although there were a few Catholics. Inner healing is a ministry little known generally in the Catholic Church except in the areas of Charismatic Renewal. Carrying out this ministry is a wonderful and humbling experience, relying entirely on the providence of the Holy Spirit for guidance and healing. Also it is exciting to see so many people recovering from depression, childhood traumas, abuse, abortions, and other traumatic situations and coming to know afresh the tremendous love that God has for them.

After this Christmas together when Peter and the rest of the family had returned to England, I went on to meet Father Robin in New York. He had been on a sabbatical in Albuquerque for six months studying with Richard Rohr, a Franciscan priest, and had taken a break over Christmas with friends just outside New York. We then flew together to Albuquerque where I stayed a few days at Tepeyak the residence for the interns of Richard Rohr's course at the Centre for Action and Contemplation, where Father Robin had been living, a lovely house where I made some good friends that I still keep. We then went up into the mountains to Pecos, New Mexico, to the Benedictine Monastery. Our Archbishop of Southwark at

the time paid all my expenses. Father Robin and I had worked together in the healing and inner healing prayer ministry for over ten years. Father Robin was very gifted by the Holy Spirit in this ministry. I had felt the Lord drawing me into this work since my experience in 1977. I had studied counselling and prayer ministry with Father Jim McManus in Perth earlier. A long time had been spent discerning whether the Lord really was calling me to go to Pecos. I was helped to do this by my own spiritual director and a very spiritually gifted priest. It was for me an incredible time. Not only did I make new friends but the whole experience was uplifting and renewing. We studied hard and received excellent spiritual direction, we kept fit, hiked in the mountains in the snow, (I took my walking boots with me) and had a lot of fun. It was a great place to be, with renewed Christian (Catholic) thinking and teaching and excellent food. There were sixty five people on the course, many of them priests or ministers of other denominations. All of us were involved in ministry in one way or another.

During the time we were away from England Ken was now always looked after in the Browside Nursing Home in Purley. Many of my friends who he knew well visited him and took him out and he still could celebrate his regular Mass on Thursday and Sunday mornings and Saturday evening with the loyal help in the nursing home and our team of helpers from the church. I phoned Ken often to reassure him that all would be well, and I also wrote all my news to him. Considering everything, he managed very well and I know that it was good for the growth of his independence. Peter of course also visited and kept an eye that everything was going okay during my absence.

Since September 1991 I had been using a room in the convent at

Orpington all day on Wednesdays and on Thursday afternoons in order to carry out the counselling and prayer ministry which I had been asked to do. Until Father Robin started his year's sabbatical, and the new parish priest came, I had been using the priest's house at Orpington continuing the work that I had been doing with Father Robin. I had also willingly taken on the people that he was leaving who still needed inner healing and help. He had arranged my transfer to the convent. I was given a key by the Sister who was in charge. It was a pleasant arrangement, and I was very happy there. I would take a picnic lunch and drive out into the country for an hour or so at lunchtime to have a break and I made good friends with the sisters. Everything worked well.

When I returned from the course for Spiritual Direction in Pecos I carried on as usual. On Thursdays I would leave Orpington about 5.45 pm and on the way home would stop at the parade of shops on the roundabout which led up to New Addington. This shop had been recommended to me about two years before by my friend Marie, who was bed bound with multiple sclerosis for many years. Her husband bought their supper at this place once every week. (Marie sadly died in 1994). It was a fish and chip shop and had won a prize. The fish was certainly beautifully cooked. Ken usually did not like fish but always enjoyed the rock salmon, and Peter liked the cod or haddock. At this time on Mondays and Wednesdays Ken was taken to La Retraite Convent at Clapham where they looked after him for the day. The authorities insisted that it was very important for all of us, so that I had some free time.

During June Peter said to me he would like to have a change from fish and chips. He said he didn't exactly have indigestion but

just a feeling when he swallowed it down, particularly the chips. I didn't get any more and changed from then on to something else. I made fish in a sauce with mashed potatoes for Peter on Thursdays and usually a burger or some sort of meat for Ken as he didn't like fish in a sauce, and all seemed well for a while. Celia and their boys, Peter junior and Mark arrived from Ottawa without Gerry for a holiday at the end of July and Paul had a barbecue party to say goodbye to everyone before he and Jane went to Africa for a year. Plans had been changed at the last moment because Jane had to have an emergency operation for appendicitis. She was in hospital and it was a busy time for Paul as he had farewell parties and events at Peper Harrow where he had been working for three years. However Jane made an extremely quick recovery, even managing to go to Paul Dufton and Linda's wedding less than a week after the operation, although I know she felt very weak.

Clare and Jonathan joined in with Paul and Jane's farewell barbecue to celebrate their engagement. It was a grand affair in the garden of Paul's cottage in Godalming. He had set up a marquee, with lighting and three big barbecues and two small ones. Everybody brought food to cook and Jane and Clare and I provided desserts and other tasties, it was a wonderful evening. Clare made a big cake in the shape of Africa, with all the countries in shapes of different colours. Peter seemed fine; he was eating and well, although now that I think about it, he could still have been feeling the discomfort and not told me. That would be in character!

On the 10th August a family group met at Clare's flat in Sunninghill made up of Peter and myself, Celia, Peter junior and Mark, Paul and Jane, and Clare and Jonathan. We all prepared something

for a picnic, and went to Windsor Great Park. We shared our lunches, it was really enjoyable and in the afternoon we went to Windsor Castle. I did not know at the time exactly what had happened to Peter at lunch time; I saw him stretching out and screwing up his face and asked him what was the matter. After he had recovered he said it was nothing, and he carried on as if nothing was the matter. Afterwards he told me that he had had an excruciating pain whilst eating a sandwich. I persuaded him to go to the doctor which he did. Dr. Till gave him some tablets to take and said come back if you have any more trouble. The tablets were for heartburn and indigestion. Peter went on as usual making no fuss or complaining and not wanting to talk about it. It seemed not to bother him any more. How was I to know that it was not alright? I asked him how he was, and he said he was okay, so I believed him.

On the 8th October, Peter had already retired from work when I invited Mary Royall to lunch with five friends from her UCM at Maresfield. Mary used to come to our Thursday morning prayer group until she moved to Maresfield. She was the friend who had helped me so much one day when Ken was impossible to manage. The group of them came to 10.00 am Mass at which Ken always presided, with either Peter or one of the helpers beside him, and then they came on to the prayer group. I had prepared lunch for about twenty-three of us, and several people made things to help out. Paddy lent us the beautiful ceramic punch bowl which her daughter Sheelagh, a contemplative nun, had made when she was working on the pottery at her convent in Northern Spain. We made a gorgeous non-alcoholic punch to serve to anyone who preferred it to wine. Helen took the day off to come and Bridget managed to get here from school for a long lunch hour. Betty came and several who were not regulars like Mary's older friend from Coulsdon, Eileen Wright, who was then eighty five. Barbara collected her and she was really pleased to be with us for lunch and of course Ken was with us as well.

Peter was busy pouring wine and looking after everybody, and so was I. Eventually I had some lunch and sat down with the others. I did not really see Peter eating but thought he had done the same. I do not monitor his every move, and I had certainly never had to encourage him to eat. The guests were spread between the two rooms and in the hall where I had put the long white sofa and a table as there was quite a crowd of us. In the evening Ken had a small meal and Peter said he was not hungry. I also wasn't hungry so I took no notice. On Friday Peter usually fasted, and would have a small piece of toast and cheese, very often while I was still bathing Ken which I did at that time on Friday mornings. The bath would take about two hours as on Fridays Ken would stay a little longer in bed. He also always washed his face and shaved before his bath which also took him quite a long time because he liked to pray and sing hymns while he shaved. Again I didn't notice anything unusual. Peter's habit was to cook egg and bacon after midnight on Friday and because I felt tired I did not wait up for him.

It was during the night on Friday the 9th October 1992 that he got up to go to the toilet and fainted, and felt very ill. I was very worried as I know that Peter is usually quite well and that when he is not he makes very little fuss, everything with him is low key. I went to Mass at 8.00 am and went straight on to the surgery which opens at 8.30. I wanted to contact Dr. Till and not someone who knew nothing about Peter. I saw Dr. Till almost immediately; he was taking his surgery in a Portakabin at the back of the new house the practice had just moved to, in order that alterations could be made. He said he could come and see Peter in the afternoon, but that if I could get him in the car even in his pyjamas, he could see him immediately. Saturday was always only for emergencies at the surgery.

When I got home, Peter said he was feeling much better. He told me then, that because this pain had returned in his digestive tract he could not eat, and had not eaten since Wednesday. I think it was a combination of weakness from not eating, and the pain. He was actually having great difficulty in getting food down. Was it some sort of obstruction or ulcer? Was it cancer? I felt this horror confirmed in me from the way he had behaved. If he had not thought it was something serious he would have told me. He was obviously afraid. He got dressed quickly and I drove him to the surgery. We went straight in to Doctor Till.

Peter told the whole story to Dr. Till with quite a lot of prompting from me. He is very reticent to talk about himself. Was it hiatus hernia? Was it an ulcer? Dr. Till asked Peter some questions and Peter told him we had arranged to go to Sorrento in Italy in nine days. I could not resist asking was it cancer, but of course got no reply. Dr. Till booked him in for an endoscopy at Mayday Hospital, prescribed him some Gaviscon and Losec tablets, and told him to go to Italy and enjoy it. He said the Gaviscon would smooth down his eating, whatever it was and make it easier. I was unhappy going off to Italy not knowing what the matter was. I tried to persuade Peter to have an endoscopy privately at St. Anthony's hospital at

Cheam, or at Shirley Oaks. He refused point blank as we have a pact that we won't have private treatment ever, but will stay on the NHS. We have always thought it unfair that we should be privileged. We wanted to put our trust in God that he would look after us. It was very difficult. I was ready to change my conviction for Peter, but afterwards felt ashamed.

I spoke to Clare about the possibilities of cancer. She panicked on the phone and said "Mummy, get it done quickly, don't waste time like happened to me." However, after one minute she phoned back to say "Delete the last conversation, I am panicking and not looking in the right direction. We must trust in God. Go on holiday, and let us calm down." I also phoned Gerard and Celia in Ottawa, and Christopher who was then back in Nicaragua. They wanted to know if they should return home, and I said that it was pointless at that moment, but they all promised to pray. Peter began to eat quite normally again and felt well, with the help of the Gaviscon and Losec, and we continued to prepare for the holiday.

On Saturday the 17th October, two days before we were due to go to Italy on the Monday, Ken returned from saying the 6.30 pm Mass with his helper. Clare and Jonathan had just arrived. Ken came in and gave me the newsletter and said hello to Clare and Jonathan. He said to me that he had felt peculiar when he got out of the car. As Ken often said he felt peculiar and was unable to distinguish symptoms or seriousness it was difficult to know clearly what really was the matter. I asked him if he thought it was a little fit, and would he like to come and sit down with us for a while. He said no, and confirmed that he was alright, and went upstairs as I went into the lounge; Clare and Jonathan were still in the hall. Ken was half way up the stairs when he let out an almighty yell... M..U..M..M..Y... and crashed backwards headfirst down the stairs, hitting his head on a glass dish which held a plant on the window-sill, taking a lump out of the paint-work. He landed with head down and feet up the stairs, in a limp mass. I ran but fortunately was not in time to break his fall, or I think I would have been hurt as well. It would all have been worse. His left eye which never closed was staring and he looked dead. He could not see or hear. I yelled for someone to dial 999 for an ambulance; they were all behind me and Peter was already at the telephone. I yelled to Clare to bring a cushion which I carefully put under his head. I didn't move him as I didn't know if anything was broken. When Ken fell it was usually like a baby and he only got bruised without broken bones. I stayed by him reassuring him, although he wasn't conscious.

The ambulance arrived in five minutes. I remember saying thank you to the Lord for the speed. They gently moved me away and took over, testing Ken's limbs, and they lifted him, sitting him on the stairs and then into their carrying chair. He looked a bit better and we could see there were no broken bones. He was completely concussed and didn't know anything or understand. I went with him in the ambulance and Peter followed in the car. Ken tried to talk, asking and asking where he was, but not understanding what I was saying. I was very worried as his brain was already very badly damaged. He did not remember anything about what happened until much later in Mayday A & E department.

The ambulance men went straight in with him while we waited in the casualty waiting room. After a while they came to tell us we could go in with him. He was still not 'with it'. We were there from 8.00 pm to 2.30 am. After a while Peter went home to have a rest. The doctors had given Ken a preliminary examination but there was nothing immediate that they could do. His head was grazed and bleeding but they had to wait to see how he recovered. The casualty department was busy. One man was very disruptive; another was difficult and kept getting off his trolley and wandering about looking in all the cubicles and saying rude things. Before we left there was a big fracas and about three police cars full of policemen and women arrived and marched through the department. I couldn't see what happened. Clare and Jonathan came to keep me company for a little while; they had actually come over to see us and have a chat before we went to Italy!! Ken didn't recognise Jonathan at all and did not know who he was!!! About 2.00 am the doctor examined Ken again. By this time he was quite lucid and wanted to know every detail of what had happened. The doctor said he did not think that Ken had fractured his skull and gave me a page of instructions for the next 24 hours. If he was sick or felt ill I was to take him back immediately. I told the doctor we were supposed to be going to Italy on Monday, although at this stage I was beginning to doubt it. The doctor assured me that if he wasn't sick or ill he would be okay to fly. Ken was anxious to get home. He was hungry and wanted a cigarette. All I had managed to get him was a glass of water. He didn't want tea from the machine. I phoned Peter and he came to collect us. Ken had a small sandwich and a cup of tea. I tucked him up in bed with instructions to call me if he felt sick or ill, or if he couldn't sleep. Amazingly he had no headache. I really praised and thanked the Lord. His head was bleeding and badly grazed, but not cut. He was bruised particularly at the bottom of his back and he felt rather stiff, otherwise he seemed alright.

In the morning I phoned Father Pat to tell him that Ken would not be saying Mass at midday, but I had to leave a message with Emily. It got a bit distorted and the congregation thought Ken was still in hospital and I had several phone calls enquiring how he was. He got up and had breakfast, washed, shaved and got dressed. He felt bruised but not too bad. He ate a good dinner and decided that he would be quite all right to fly to Italy the next day even though he felt stiff and bruised. During the morning on Sunday I remembered how Isabel, a good friend from the prayer group, had told me of the wonders of Arnica tablets. She said she always kept them in the house for her family. She had used them when they were bruised at sports or when they had teeth out; she had they reduced pain and swelling like a miracle. I decided to phone Isabel about 11.30 am; she had just bought a new bottle of the tablets and would bring them over immediately after lunch. She came at 2.00 pm and I started giving them to Ken every hour. They worked like a miracle certainly and he suffered no pain at all from the fall. He could not do up his shoes for several days and his bottom was a bit sore, but the result was amazing.

We had a good week in Italy. Ken was cooperative, as much anyway as he could be, and I was watching Peter like a hawk. He was taking the Gaviscon and Losec and eating bravely. He had difficulty with some foods, particularly pasta, but he usually makes very little fuss anyway. We couldn't hire a wheelchair for Ken as we had planned to do. No one in Italy seemed to know what a wheelchair was, even though Peter speaks Italian fluently. Our courier also tried hard to locate one. We guessed the hospitals had them but they would not lend them. This meant that I had to hold on to Ken all the time, except when he walked up and down on the terrace of the hotel, he always felt insecure anyway on new territory. There were times when this was quite tiring as we covered a lot of ground one way and another. For instance at Herculaneum, although we had a hired car, which we were able to park right at the entrance, there was a walk of about half a mile to the actual excavations, and then one had to go down steep steps. Ken was quite happy to sit and wait while Peter and I explored further. I was practically carrying Ken on the way back. I felt protective of Peter and wouldn't let him look after Ken. I have since, without any reply, written to the Italian Ministry of Culture, suggesting that they have a couple of wheelchairs available even for the elderly at Herculaneum. It would mean that some people would be able to go round the excavations who could not manage the long walk down the road from the entrance where cars are not allowed.

We did not hire a car for the entire week but chose the three days at the end of the week; we could travel in the hotel mini-bus, and it was also quite easy to travel on the buses. The service was good from outside the hotel, although this meant a lot of pushing and pulling with Ken, getting him on and off!! It was hard on my back which is usually very strong. We could also hire a taxi quite easily.

Each day Ken sat quietly, either in a church or in the local Cathedral or by the sea to read his 'Office' for about an hour. The day we went to Sorrento in our hired car, we left him in the Carmelite church, quite happily, about 11.30 am, saying we would return in an hour and telling him not to move. We walked through the town and did some shopping. We bought some things for a picnic lunch and a drink. We enquired in one of the big hotels on the sea front up on the cliff top whether the Cocumella Hotel was still there. We were told that it most certainly was, about a kilometre along from where we were. The year before Peter and I were married, 1952, we had stayed in the Cocumella with Peter's Mum and Dad. They had invited me to join them on a holiday whilst they were on leave in England. They were between diplomatic posts in Poland and Caracas. We planned to visit the Cocumella in the afternoon in nostalgic mood, with Ken. We had found it beautiful, and remembered a lot of the experiences we had whilst there. We had walked through the orange groves in the grounds after dinner, and sat on the cliff top looking out over the Mediterranean watching the lights of the fishing boats. Another memory was Peter's Dad, Fred, walking across the beach in his wet white baggy underpants in which he had been swimming because he couldn't be bothered to put on his swimming trunks and he wanted to move into the sun from the shady rocks. He didn't worry what anyone thought. There were many stories to tell about Fred, he was a real 'character'. It took a while for me to get used to him. I had not met him until the holiday in 1952 as he had arrived in England from Poland after Peter's Mum. In that year before we went to Sorrento we had been staying in Rome, and the person who was supposed to meet us the evening we arrived was held up and did not get to the appointed place. It was Holy Year and Rome was packed with tourists and pilgrims and there were no hotel rooms free. We were booked into a flat with a maid, but did not have the address, which meant we were homeless. We managed to find an English convent where we could spend the night, which Peter's mother fortunately remembered from the time they had lived in Rome when Peter was a child. They had no real spare room in the convent. Vivien, Peter's sister, Mum and I slept in an attic with nothing in it but three hastily assembled camp beds, and a jug of water and a bowl. We had a marathon journey to the toilet. Peter and Dad were sleeping on the floor in a school nearby, and had to wash in a fountain in the quadrangle. About 3.00 am our door burst open and it was Dad who had refused to take notice of the night portress who said access to our room at night was forbidden, but he knew where we were. He said "I'm going, I can't stand this any longer," and he went. I was really worried because I thought we would lose him but Mum reassured me and said she could guess where he would be. "Best to leave him," she said in her wisdom, with years of understanding. We picked him up two days later when we had settled into our flat. He was in a first-class hotel, near where they had lived years before. Dad left Mum to pay the bill as he never carried money with him, and he walked out in a very good mood. The matter was never mentioned again by him, although we have laughed about it many times.

To revert to the earlier story, we returned in good time to the Carmelite church to collect Ken, to find the it locked and no sign of him. We had told him to stay there and not move but little dreaming it would be shut for the afternoon at midday. We pressed the bell on the Monastery door, which was fortunately by the church. A reply came through the intercom to come back after siesta at 4.30; it was a female voice. The second time we pressed the bell they said that they were having lunch and did not want to be disturbed. What a blessing that Peter speaks fluent Italian, at least we could understand. We had to press the bell three times before we could get anyone to listen to our plight, and then a Carmelite priest came and opened the door. He brought the keys and confessed to having locked Ken in. He had not got Ken to understand that he was locking the church, and insisted that he did not know what else to do but leave him locked in. Ken was actual_y horrified when he heard the door lock and realised that he could not get out and that we could not get in. In the end it all turned out well. This priest had only been in Sorrento for three days and was afraid of not carrying out his duties. He was actually very nice when he had got over his confusion and upset, especially when he found that Ken was a priest. Fortunately Ken was remarkably calm. I think when he saw us he was okay and felt safe. We managed to combine our chat to the priest with a visit to the sacristy toilet, so all was well. I had always impressed on Ken that whatever happened or wherever he was, I would always find him and he really believed this, which was a blessing.

When in the afternoon we found the Cocumella we were unable to go in as there was a wedding party having photos taken in the foyer, but we did walk through the orange groves to the cliff top. There were tables set out in beautiful pink for the wedding guests in an ideal situation on the cliff overlooking the sea. We felt we had better not stay too long as Ken had chosen to wait in the car and we had already been asked if we were guests at the wedding as we parked.

When we got home from Italy we had only a short time to wait for Peter's appointment at Mayday Hospital on 17th November. I tried again to get him to go privately but he refused. I am sure this was right in the end. One cannot change a principle to suit one's convenience and for myself I know this, but found it more difficult to keep the principle for Peter. We are totally under the NHS, and are very satisfied although we see that many changes need to be made. We kept our appointment at Mayday Hospital for the endoscopy and afterwards Mr Wickers the consultant told Peter he would most probably have to have an operation. We did not know more than this but Peter was given appointments for the following day to have blood tests, an X-ray, and an ultra-sound scan, so we knew it was serious. It was on the 30th November we had an appointment to see Mr Wickers to hear exactly what was wrong. He explained that Peter had a growth in and around his oesophagus. He didn't mention the dreaded word 'cancer' so I asked him, "Is it cancer?" He said "Yes, it is an adeno-carcinoma." He went on to explain that Peter would have at least sixteen weeks chemotherapy or possibly more, and if the tumour shrank there would be an operation. He started to tell us that it was a very difficult and serious operation, and that Peter would have to rest after his meals because eating would become difficult. He realized that we were shocked and unable to take in any more than the immediate news. He arranged to make an appointment with Dr. David Cunningham, an oncologist at the Royal Marsden. Dr. Cunningham was the consultant Clare was under since the sad death of 'Big Mac' who had helped her so much. He had been strongly criticised in the press for his attitude to the Bristol experiment and had committed suicide.

David Cunningham was a youngish man, who gave the impression of knowing what he was doing and we had great confidence in him. Our appointment with him was made very quickly as Mr Wickers had said, so we knew how serious Peter's condition was. When the appointment letter arrived Peter dealt with it and wrote the day on the calendar. He told me it was the next Wednesday. When we arrived at the hospital I felt the receptionist's surprise, but she asked us to sit down. After a little while she came over and said "I'm really sorry but your appointment is not until next week." When Peter looked again at the letter he could see that it said Wednesday the 16th and not the 9th. He had been so desperate to come that he had thought it was the first Wednesday. We were distraught as we had hoped to get everything settled and I drove him home with both of us in tears. We sat on the sofa and held each other and cried and cried. Then we talked non-stop for about three hours about death and facing illness, and what it was all about. This was a healing afternoon. We both felt much better and it helped us to remember to focus our sights on Jesus, and to trust day by day, although this was not always easy.

When we got to the appointment the next week, we were much more ready to hear what Dr Cunningham said, as he explained all the details and we were able to ask the questions we needed to ask, also to make the decisions we had to make. He explained the seriousness of the situation and told us that it was vital that the tumour shrank before an operation was possible. He said this type of tumour, an adeno-carcinoma, could not be got rid of by chemotherapy, but the chemotherapy sometimes, in a small number of patients, enabled the operation to take place, and that was the only purpose of it. He explained that there were two protocols to choose from, their own local treatment known as 'ECF' and what he said was the best alternative known as 'FAMTX.' There was as yet nothing to prove one was better than the other. The regimen ECF stands for the three drugs that are given - EPIRUBICIN, CISPLATIN and 5-FLUOROURACIL (5FU). The 5FU is given into a vein under the collar bone, through a plastic tube called a Hickman line. This line stays in place under the skin for the duration of the treatment (usually 18 weeks) but in Peter's case it was 21 weeks as his tumour was very advanced. The chemo is pumped in 24 hours a day using a motorised pump which is worn round the waist. This was very different from the method employed at the Marsden for many cancer patients when Clare was there. The other two treatments are given either overnight as an in-patient, or all day as a day-patient, every three weeks for a total of six treatments. The alternative treatment called FAMTX is a combination of Methotrexate, 5 Fluorouracil, Andriamycin and Folinic acid. The Methotrexate is given in a high dosage to activate the 5FU. 24 hours later the antidote (folinic acid) is given to minimise the side effects of the treatment. The last drug, Andriamycin is given two weeks after the first part of the treatment. This treatment would cycle every 28 days and would not need a Hickman line. The side effects of both would be the same, that is, mouth ulcers, diarrhoea, skin rash, nausea and vomiting and the loss of hair.

Dr. Cunningham explained exactly where the cancer was by drawing the digestive tract on the roll of blue paper which pulled over the examination couch for hygiene so that it was clean for each patient. It was very descriptive and helped me to understand more clearly. Peter had to choose which protocol he would follow, an impossible decision as we knew and understood so little about it all. In the end Dr. Cunningham said he would choose the EFC for Peter. My prayer was, "Lord, we are in your hands, please see that the chemotherapy, backed by your love and power, shrinks the tumour, so that Peter will be healed and that glory is given to you." First of all Peter was nervous but light hearted. When he realized it was actually cancer his shock started to show. He found it difficult to sleep and was obviously suffering a great deal in his innermost being. He wanted to go to Burrswood for healing prayer. This was the last time he drove the car until he was quite better. Clare and Jonathan came with us, for which I was really grateful. Peter having said he knew the way, got lost and became like a madman, driving round the lanes at high speed and nothing would stop him. I could see the tremendous tension in him. I think that Clare and Jonathan thought they would not get back alive. When we arrived there was a long service going on followed by a healing service and Peter had some prayer from a very understanding minister. I think it helped him a great deal.

Peter went through a deep dark night of the soul during this time, partly from the torture going on in his mind and partly the battle for control... wanting to give in and surrender and to let things take their place and to go the way the Lord wants versus the need to stay in control and have things the way they have always been. This dark night lasted quite a long time. Peter went through a deep repentance for many things, with many tears. He said sorry for all the years he had smoked and for his weakness and inability to give up. He said sorry for the times that he had filled his subsistence forms in creatively for the office when he had been abroad. Everyone did it so that the most money could be claimed. This worried him so much that he tried to pay back what he thought he had received dishonestly but no one wanted to know these facts, so he sent a £1,000 cheque to the Civil Service Welfare Association. Many other things happened at this time. Sometimes he would clutch me in a desperate manner and say I am in a dark void, there is nothing. He would shout, as much as he ever could

shout, "Darling, don't leave me, don't ever leave me, it is terrible."
All I could do was to hold him and pray.

Waiting for the chemotherapy to start was the worst time. Dr.
Till had told Peter that at the Marsden they did not always spell
everything out and that the chemotherapy was worse than they
said. I am not sure that this was a wise statement, but it was most
probably true. During this time I had not been well, I guess mostly
it was tension. Doctor Phillips helped me a lot; she listened to me
and was extremely understanding and my tension released. When
I saw that Peter was so bad I seemed to get a new strength and an
ability to put my trust totally in God, and I felt wonderfully well
despite everything.

For the last ten years Peter and I had been running 'Life in the
Spirit Seminars' in the diocese whereever we were invited. We had
carried out a new form of these seminars in Tunbridge Wells
during the September of 1992. Although the cancer must have
been growing since the beginning of the year or longer, or so the
doctors thought, Peter had written and planned these seminars
extremely well, and had seemed very fit. He had condensed the
seven week seminars into five consecutive nights to suit the
requirements of the prayer group and the parish council at
Tunbridge Wells, and it seemed successful. With our team of
helpers and music ministry we hosted 250 people. We know that
numbers do not denote success really, but there was such a
response that during October Peter wrote an article about it for the
'Good News' magazine at the request of Kristina Cooper, the
editor. At the end of the article Peter offered to send a copy of
the five day seminars to anyone who wanted it if they sent a large

SAE. The response was amazing and as Peter sent out the copies, he put in a note to say that he had just found out that he had cancer of the oesophagus and would the recipients pray for him. We were inundated with cards, Masses, phone calls, and promises of prayer. It was marvellous to have so many people praying. I had written letters to inform everyone who I knew prayed, about Peter's situation. This included most of the people on the course with me in the USA, as well as Father Andrew, who I had known well during my stay at the monastery at the beginning of 1992, and who had been made Abbot in the last year. He recommended an excellent book about cancer which helped me to pray for Peter. He promised to ask all the community to pray each day. I wrote to a friend in Italy and the entire Australian contingent and of course our own family, prayer groups and parish. This made a tremendous difference to me. I felt really supported after a very groggy start, and was able to be very positive in the Lord's strength.

I wrote at this time:-
"Father, I feel a great light shining today. I know I am in it, and I feel Lord, that you are already healing Peter. Maybe we both have a great deal of healing to go through. I feel you are calling us to understand other people at a deeper level, and to know what it is you want us to do. There must be more to it all. I do know that cancer is not of you and that you want to heal. Jesus came to show who you are, and Jesus also healed all those who came to him. Jesus I believe you are alive now, risen and here. We come to you for healing. We praise and thank you for loving us and for wanting us to be healed I believe you want to heal Peter. Thank you, thank you, thank you."

Chapter Fifteen

Clare's Wedding

All this time, preparations were going on non-stop for Clare's wedding. The date had been fixed a year beforehand for the 1st May 1993, long before the first signs of Peter's illness. We had then booked the banqueting hall at the Council Offices where Peter and I had the reception for our own wedding in 1953. We had tried to book somewhere recommended by Betty and David of Harvey's who were going to do the catering, and who we knew well and trusted. This had more pleasant surroundings and a terrace, but it was fully booked for May. We had a family conference when Peter became ill and we were not sure how things would be, or whether in actual fact Peter would be well enough to attend the wedding. After the start of his treatment it seemed possible that he would manage it. He had some days each three weeks when although he felt weak and his mind was not very clear, he was reasonably active. The doctors at the Royal Marsden had said they would do everything to help him to be there.

Clare arranged for her wedding dress to be made at Jennifer's. She was a couturier who had opened a business in Purley the week Clare was looking for a dressmaker designer. Jennifer was talented, and although we did not have any recommendations beforehand, Clare had a big hunch that she was the right person, and indeed she was. She herself became pregnant a few months before Clare's wedding and whether she could not manage financially or was not well we do not know. The premises were seen to be closed one day, about a year later. Jennifer designed and fitted Clare and Marjorie her assistant did the sewing. They were both extremely talented and knowledgeable.

Clare would come over to us every so often for a fitting and we would shop and arrange all the things that needed doing. Peter helped choose the invitations and other wedding stationery and I set about painting a cover for the service booklets with the Mass details for each of the guests. Father Robin had promised that he would celebrate the wedding Mass which he did, although unbeknown to us the trauma had started which led to his abandonment of his vows and his eventual marriage in October 1994.

This was all kept hidden from me because of Peter's illness for which I suppose I am grateful. The first I knew was when Robin came especially to see me in January 1994 when Peter was really recovering from his operation. He was in turmoil; I listened to him for three hours and then I heard no more until April, when he phoned on a Friday just after Easter to say that he was 'leaving his church' on Sunday afternoon. Although of course I know we are all free to do what we choose, it was a very sad day, and I guess I said some things which are true but that he didn't like. He has had very little contact with me since, and I guess after all those years working with him as a priest I would find it too difficult, so it is most probably a blessing. However the Lord knows that I wish him well and want for him everything that the Lord wants for him. When Peter became very ill in April, I really began to wonder what would happen because the wedding was only three weeks away. Notes from my diary:

Thursday 3rd April 1993
Peter had his fifth treatment today. All went well. The doctor had previously put him on steroids with something else to ease the sickness and he seemed a little better though it is still all traumatic.

Peter cannot manage to flush his Hickman line, his hands shake and he gets panicky. Even when he has to switch the alarm off when things aren't working properly his hands shake so much he has difficulty. Each Wednesday and Saturday I have already been scrubbing up, putting on medical rubber gloves and preparing everything but I have found now that I have to do the whole thing and risk any cross infection. Peter just cannot do it. It is a very fiddly business and requires endless washing of hands and being very fussy. He just hates the whole thing.

As his hair is now very thin it has been suggested amongst his nurses and carers that he gets a wig. He is not very keen but with Clare's wedding coming up next month he was persuaded. The doctors say they can postpone his treatment at that time so that he is feeling as well as possible.

Also we have been told we can seal off the Hickman line whilst he is at the wedding and the reception and open it again in the evening. It means he will not have to wear the pump and the chemo bag. It will be a great relief for him and he will be able to wear his morning suit with no lumps and bumps. He does so want to be well enough to take an active part and I do pray that he will. We are going to Rose Hill tomorrow to the wig maker.

Friday 4th April 1993

We have been to Rose Hill today. Everything was extremely difficult It was I am sure too soon after Peter's treatment. He so wants to get on with things and be well. He has been very confused and found having the wig fitted traumatic. He was feeling rotten. We left everything and came home.

Saturday 5th April 1993

Peter was very sick today. We should have been going to the Fairfield Halls tonight but Peter was too ill and went to bed.

Sunday 6th April 1993

Peter lay on the bed all day. He had nothing to eat. All he wants is grapefruit juice and milk shakes, which he has not previously liked. I was so worried about Peter's condition that I phoned the Marsden. Lorraine, his special nurse told me to get in touch with Peter's own doctor and phone her back with the results.

Monday 7th April 1993

I phoned the surgery urgently and asked for Doctor Till to visit. He came almost immediately with a student. Peter was in bed and almost non-compos. I told the doctor about his thirst and he said it was most probably the chemo had caused it. When I phoned back and told Lorraine the details, she said "Bring him in straight away". Fortunately Christopher was with me at home, and between us we managed to get Peter into his dressing gown and into the car. He was not able to do anything for himself. He was examined immediately by Dr Tim Jones and Dr Ellis the senior registrar at that time. Lorraine could see immediately that something was very wrong. As the doctors spoke to Peter with rather loud commanding voices, asking his name, he recognised them and seemed to perk up. He then strangely started getting stroppy with me. He said he was quite okay and that there was no need to make such a fuss. ....the two doctors decided to take him off the chemo. They shut off the Hickman line and removed the bag and the pump. It was by now late afternoon. Chris was still with me. The hospital pharmacy was closed so they had to go round the wards to find the medication they wanted Peter to take. They told me to bring Peter back on the following Tuesday, a whole week. I not only felt worried about Peter being so ill but was worried about him missing a week of the chemotherapy. I knew I had to trust in the doctors as well as God. It was difficult.

Tuesday 8th April 1993
Peter did not sleep all night, consequently neither did I. Peter continues to be very thirsty, almost demanding milkshakes, quite out of character. I was doing my best to look after him, and I was praying constantly for guidance. I felt very frightened. Peter was just lying in bed, totally confused and floppy and really quite out of his mind. He was very ill, certainly worse than he had been at the hospital. He couldn't talk and was drinking anything I would give him. I felt pleased about this as he had had nothing to eat; I was at least giving him nourishing milk shakes, or so I thought.

During the afternoon he continued to get worse. I was so glad Christopher was with me. Peter did not know what he was doing and I could not leave him. We were both very worried, but I was waiting for the medication the doctors had given him to work. It was in the early hours of the morning when Christopher said to me, "I think Daddy is dying, I have never seen anyone so ill," I knew he was right. I immediately phoned the Marsden and spoke to Doctor Alexander, who was on night duty. I told him the whole story and the symptoms. He said that it was most probably to do with the leucocytes, or something that I did not understand, and said that it would come right. He said there was no one there at the moment who could do anything but that I was to phone Pinkham in the morning when they opened at 8.00 am. Chris and I had no sleep for the rest of the night. I dared not go to sleep in case Peter got out of bed. He kept wandering about and I was afraid he would fall. His mind was completely unconscious although his body was working.

In the morning I phoned Pinkham at 7.40 am and spoke to Lorraine, who was the sister on duty. I thanked God it was her, because she knew all about Peter and understood. Straight away, she said to bring Peter in. It is impossible to get an ambulance to the Marsden; if you call you are automatically taken to Mayday. I knew this from previous occasions. There was nothing for it but to get Peter down the stairs and into the car. By now he was completely unconscious in body and mind, and very floppy. Chris and I could not lift him between us. We had a real job to get his dressing gown on him. We then dragged him in a blanket across the bedroom and slid him down the stairs. We put Chris' car as near as we could to the front door and pushed and pulled till we could get him on to the back seat. I arranged lots of pillows round him, so that he would not hurt himself and tucked a blanket over him. He was sprawled across the seat and I had to hold him in with my foot in order to shut the car door. It was a terrible ordeal, although Peter himself was fortunately unaware.

On arrival at the Marsden we got him into a wheelchair with a lot of help from people around, and took him up to Pinkham in the lift, in spite of the fact that he kept sliding out of the wheelchair. Lorraine had alerted the doctors who had seen him on Monday, and they were waiting.

Doctor Tim Jones examined him, trying unsuccessfully to rouse him and then they quickly started extensive tests. They told me it was one of three things; diabetes was one, I cannot remember the others. By midday they had confirmed that it was diabetes and that it was serious. His blood count was the highest they had ever known. It was 76. He was immediately put on a drip with medication. I think it was insulin, but they might have started him on something else. I was in quite a state and was listening but not taking everything in. I was also very tired.

Peter was then transferred to a trolley and taken to Kennaway Ward, where he had previously had his first two nightly chemo treatments. It was Wednesday in Holy Week, and Peter remained totally unconscious until 4.00 am. on Maundy Thursday morning, when he answered the Sister, but even this he didn't remember afterwards. The Sister was so delighted that she phoned me at 8.00 am to tell me that Peter had spoken. They had been very worried that he would not recover from the coma; this was the first sign of hope. Chris had gone home in the morning to see that Ken was alright and to have a rest and I spent my time during the next days popping home to Ken to look after him, to do the jobs that were essential and sitting beside Peter and praying.

When I visited Peter on Maundy Thursday morning, he was slightly more conscious, but still quite dulally, and I was very worried for his mental health. It was quite frightening. They could only give him insulin very slowly because of his condition, so his blood sugar level, although lower than before was still very high. It was Good Friday morning when Peter started to come back to life. Although he was not completely lucid he was beginning to talk more normally. The dietician had been to see him to explain what diabetes was and to say he was being put on a special diet with no sugar. He had his eyes open but was not taking things in.

I am not sure what happened but I arrived to find him just about to tuck into a slice of lemon meringue pie. Because he had not been able to order his meal the day before the ward maid gave him a choice of dessert not realising he was not allowed sugar. He was very disappointed when he had the lemon meringue taken away and still could not understand that he had diabetes. I realised also that he had not understood why they were pricking his finger every hour and testing his blood. It was in the night on Good Friday that he really became much better and his blood sugar reading was down to 13, which is still very high comparatively. It should be about 5 or so, but he was quite lucid.

On Saturday when I knew that Peter was going to be better, and he was understanding what was going on, I left the hospital about 9.30 and went to church for the Easter Vigil. I had asked Father Salmon to ask people to pray particularly for the diabetes to be healed as many of the congregation were gathered for the Holy Week services. They were all already praying for the healing of Peter's oesophageal cancer. At the end of the long and very beautiful Mass everyone gathered round to know how Peter was, and were overjoyed to hear that he was over the worst.

On Sunday I was able to bring him home. He was put back on the Hickman line, pump, and chemo. We then started the diet and the two hourly finger prick and test.

Chris was so good and helpful at this time. It just happened that he was staying at home during the Easter holiday whilst he was studying at Lancaster University for his degree in information systems. He not only supported me and came to the hospital to see Peter, but helped me look after Ken. The others were all further away. Gerard of course was in Canada. Clare and Jonathan came over a lot to support me and to see Peter, the phone was ringing all day with Paul and Gerard and others enquiring how Peter was.

I asked how it was that the two doctors who had examined Peter on Friday had not diagnosed diabetes earlier. They were rather ashamed to say and very apologetic that, although they had taken a blood test, which I knew, the lab did not have a routine test for diabetes. They have now included it on a regular basis.

This spell of unusual diabetes lasted until Peter was tested again in August when the chemotherapy was finished and his blood sugar was found to be quite normal. The doctors said the cause was a quirk of the treatment.

While Peter had been so ill, all the arrangements for Clare's wedding were still going ahead. We had already been to Moss Bros in Croydon to get him fitted for a morning suit. We took with us at the same time all the measurements for those who could not come for a fitting because they were either abroad or living away from us, this included Gerry in Canada, Steve in New York, Chris who was in Lancaster and Paul and Jonathan looked after their own where they were. Clare's flowers were decided and were to be delivered. I took on the decorating of the Council Offices' banqueting hall where the reception was to take place. This posed a few problems which were solved both by Pam who owned the florist at the bottom of Old Lodge Lane, and by a night raid on Bridget's garden for greenery. Pam had some ideas and was willing to go in first thing in the morning on the day. There was a long sweeping staircase which in the end looked lovely. Bridget brought the pew end decorations from the church and hung them, and Pam produced some entwining greenery etc.

Peter found everything very tiring and we made sure he had no feeling of responsibility. I knew that we could rely on Betty and David our caterers to do everything very well. We had been into some detail with them earlier and Betty, understanding the situation completely, took over and it was all done beautifully.

On the morning of the wedding I had to give quite a lot of time to getting Peter and Ken ready, with a visit to the banqueting hall to put out the flowers I had arranged, and take the last few things. Unfortunately this meant that Clare did not get all the attention that she should have had. I was very conscious of this. I had planned my own getting ready to require the minimum of time. My clothes were laid out ready, and my hair was done the day before. It meant that Clare and her number one bridesmaid Jenny were left to answer the door, and I know she did not have as much time as she would have liked. Also we were all tired.

However it was amazing that we managed to get it all done, Celia and Gerry and Peter junior and Mark, stayed several nights in Josie's house in West Croydon, and Josie went to stay with Marion in West Wickham, which was kind of her, as there was not really room in our house. All the boys went to a local hotel, which took some pressure off us, so that there was then plenty of room for Jenny and Clare's cousin Madeleine, who brought her youngest daughter Joanne over in the morning, she was eleven and also a bridesmaid.

Clare and Jonathan had chosen an open-topped 1931 'Old Crock' for their wedding car. It was in lovely condition and cared for by an ardent adorer owner. We had tested it out one day in December, in snow, with a bitterly cold wind. Everyone loved it, and it really stole the show. I can remember arriving at the church and greeting the visitors, and then sitting in the front waiting for Clare, thanking God that all was alright. Peter looked marvellous considering the trauma. Most of his hair had come out, but new hair had grown up underneath. He did not need the wig. He was very thin and his suit rather hung on him but he looked quite smart.

The wedding was a wonderful affair. Jonathan's friends from the Clifton Cathedral choir provided the music and it was superb. I think everyone enjoyed it. Bishop Howard was present on the sanctuary and five priest friends concelebrated, including Father Martin Lee, Father Pat, Robin who presided and a friend of Jonathan's family. At the time for the wedding vows, Robin invited everyone in the church to come up and gather round the altar, it was a wonderful moment. Then we had a time for prayer when Jonathan's mother and myself laid hands on Clare. I remember that Clare and I both cried profusely, although quietly, and tears streamed down our faces. Whatever this was about we don't know, but I guess that on my part it was joy and thanksgiving for Clare's life, which has been so blessed by the Lord. I have never felt that I have lost a daughter, rather gained a son.

After the photos, which took a long time, Clare and Jonathan had a wonderful send off to the reception in their open-topped car. The children (not to mention the men) loved it. People sat in it and tried it out. Clare had invited anyone from the parish who wanted to be present, to come to the church, and there were quite a lot of them. Many people in the parish knew Clare, partly because she had lived here all her life, partly because they had prayed for her for so long when she was so ill with Hodgkins disease. The other reason that she was well known was because she was one of the main organisers of the Youth Mass for several years when it had been so popular. They had always gathered together to pray before they planned the Youth Mass, and I am sure this is why it went so well. Bishop Howard had written to say he would not be able to stay to the reception but I think that he enjoyed the

Mass so much he decided to stay on. Gabrielle Culliford also stayed. She had just come to the church from Dorking to see Clare married, and had intended to go off to lunch with a friend. In the event she had tried to phone her friend, and could not make contact, so I invited her to the reception. She eventually spoke to her friend who seemed to understand. It was already late as the wedding ceremony was nearly two hours long, let alone the time for photographs. It so happened that someone who came to the wedding could not stay to the reception, so Gabrielle found herself sitting next to the Bishop, who was squeezed in at the end of a table. They got on very well and found they had a lot in common. Bridget was looking after Ken for me, and I think she had a difficult time. She must have been glad to take Ken home early so that he could have a rest before 6.30 pm Mass. Since his accident he had found ccping with large gatherings of people very difficult.

The meal was beautifully set out. The tables looked very attractive. We had all helped David the night before trying to place the tables to make room for the hundred and ten guests. It was Steve's wife Jeanette, who had come over from New York early for the wedding, who had a novel plan for arranging the tables, and from then on it was easy; everyone was so helpful. On the day itself when it came to the speeches, Peter was able to stand and speak for about five minutes and then Gerard took over with a very snappy, prepared speech on Peter's behalf. After the meal people came over to Peter to talk to him; he managed very well, surprisingly until about 11.00 pm. Instead of having a disco or some kind of dancing after the meal Clare had invited the guests to bring a song or a dance or an item to entertain everyone else.

We had a great selection of talent, including excellent comedy, song and musicians including Peter and Mark. Little Mark told a wonderful off-the-cuff story with musical accompaniments from Richard the best man who held the whole thing together musically. The choir from Clifton Cathedral, all of whom Jonathan knew well, contributed some beautiful works. On the whole it was a very friendly and enjoyable time. Even the bride sang a song with Helen and Chantal which Paul had written. Bridget had charge of the church mini-bus and brought Clare and Jonathan and several others including ourselves back to the house in an entirely untraditional manner. She was a great support. I think she must have been very tired as she did so much to help us. Clare and Jonathan then went off to the Selsdon Park Hotel, in full regalia.

I managed to get myself organised for the lunch on Sunday to which we had invited the closer family and friends, about thirty of us. It was a lovely day, and we had the video of the wedding to watch. Although it was not very professional we all enjoyed it. Peter again stood up to the strain well, just sitting quietly and letting people come to him. We were so pleased that he was able to take an active part.

Chapter Sixteen

Peter's Operation

On the 3rd June 1993 Peter completed the last treatment of the chemotherapy. It was gruelling and they had told Peter and myself that if the tumour had not shrunk sufficiently for the operation there was nothing more that they could do. He had completed the eight big treatments as well as the pump and Hickman line running in a continuous supply of 5FU. They intended to leave this for another two weeks. However, after this last treatment Peter was very ill. His digestive system was completely out of order. For two weeks he could not eat and nothing was working properly. It was as if the chemotherapy was really poisoning him. As this total breakdown took place they immediately detached the 5FU line for good.

This was a worrying time as Peter, who was already very thin, lost a lot of weight. I was afraid even if the tumour had shrunk that he would be too ill for the operation. I was really trying to trust God completely and not have negative thoughts. This was difficult but all the family were supportive. Those who were too far away to visit were closely in touch by phone. Peter had an appointment on the 15th June with Mr Wickers, for an endoscopy. We did not hear the result of this. On the 21st June Peter had a CT scan at the Royal Marsden and again no results were shared, we just had to wait. On the 28th June Peter had an appointment with the Consultant Oncologist David Cunningham. By now Peter was beginning to eat again and was feeling a little stronger. Because we had not been told the results of the scan we were very keyed up for this appointment. We had no idea whether the tumour had shrunk enough, whatever that meant, and it was a very tense time. We were trusting and praying and yet all the human feelings of wanting to know for sure were there. Somehow though, Peter and I were aware of being deeply at peace. The clinic at the Marsden was busy. We know the lounge so well where we had to wait. I have sat in it many times over the years with Clare, as well as during the last year with Peter. We still had to wait quite a long time after we went through to 'the other side.' When the time came we actually saw Dr. Mark Ellis. He told us that Dr. Cunningham was extremely busy. There was no ceremony at all. Mark Ellis said, "So, you are going to have the operation then!" We were overjoyed that the tumour had shrunk sufficiently. He said, "You are strong and healthy, your heart is good!!! Why not?" He also said he would telephone Mr Ebbs the surgeon who would carry out the operation and that we would be sent an appointment. We soon received a card inviting Peter to meet Mr. Ebbs on the 14th July.

During the last weeks of his chemotherapy, at least on the better days, Peter had been talking about having a holiday before the operation. This I think was both to recover from the trauma of the last year and partly that we could be together for a while in case the operation did not go well.

Peter fancied going to Turkey. I wrote to Maureen and Michael

O'Connor in Dublin who had enjoyed a successful holiday in Turkey and Maureen sent us a great deal of information. I was not certain about it as I was unsure how well Peter would be, and concerned about the food causing upsets to his stomach. However this idea was put on ice after the 14th July. Mr Ebbs was very pleasant but direct. He asked us if we understood why Peter was to have the operation. There was a long pause, and then I said, "Because there is no alternative. "Peter laughed and said that there was an alternative"! Mr Ebbs said, "Yes, you are right, but you wouldn't like to take it!" and we both said, "No." Mr Ebbs went on to explain that Peter's tumour was an adeno-carcinoma which was impossible to get rid of except by resection. He explained again exactly where the tumour was, and impressed on us what a difficult and dangerous operation it was, with many hazards. He told us that one in ten people die, either during or after the operation; that the eighth day was the crisis day, because a test was made then to see if the join which had been made was leak proof. He said that sometimes this took a long time to heal. He explained that even when this join had healed there were many difficulties following, not the least in learning to eat again, this would be a very slow process. He said there was much more to it but that it was "academic!" ...whatever that meant.

Mr Ebbs then showed us where Peter would be cut; a long incision would be made from below his right front rib, round the front, under his arm at lower rib level and across his back. He then explained in detail the operation. We were astonished because at this stage we knew nothing about it. He said a rib would be removed by sawing, and that they would deflate the left lung in order to reach the oesophagus which lies towards the back inside the spinal column. He said they would then remove the entire stomach, cut off the oesophagus above the tumour and join the oesophagus to the intestine which they would pull up from lower down. He did forget to tell Peter at this stage that they also would remove his spleen. When Peter found out after the operation that he also had no spleen and had to take penicillin every day of his life, he was quite upset. I am sure this is a process of real bereavement or loss after a big operation. Peter only found out about his spleen because we asked what the penicillin was for.

Mr Ebbs explained that they had tried every way and had found this the most successful. It was very difficult to join two comparatively rigid organs like the oesophagus and the stomach, and there was not room to lift the stomach into the necessary position, so even though he knew the stomach was not affected it had to be removed. Mr Ebbs then explained to Peter that he would lose at least three stones in weight and would very likely not regain any of it as of course although digestion would take place all through the digestive tract, without a stomach it would be impaired a great deal and he would not get all the nourishment he had previously. He explained it all unemotionally, and although we had some questions, again we were rather amazed at all this, and just quietly accepted it. Mr Ebbs further explained that it was important that the operation was carried out quickly as the adeno-carcinoma grew quickly and must not be left. The first day that he was free to do it was the 15th August and he asked if we would accept that. Peter said that of course he would. Mr Ebbs then told Peter to come in on Friday the 13th August for blood tests and an ECG, and at this stage some jokes were made which lightened the whole procedure. The programme would be that Peter would go in on the morning of Sunday the 15th August at 10.00 am and the operation would take place at 8.30 am on Monday morning the 16th August. Once we had seen Mr Ebbs all thought of going away for holiday left our minds. Peter just wanted to get on with the job, and indeed so did I. I strangely felt no fear, and absolute trust in Mr Ebbs who certainly gave the impression that he knew what he was doing. During this waiting period Peter became very well. He was eating heartily, and life returned to some sort of normality.

Hilary, our niece, was home from Nassau with little Danny, who had been born in April and we went over to my sister Margie's to see her. There is a lovely photograph of Peter holding Danny in which he looks very well and back to normal, in great contrast to the rather thin ill-looking Peter at Clare's wedding in May. His weight went back on quickly and by the 13th August he was almost back to 13 stones. When Martin his personal nurse weighed him he had put on 13 lbs in four weeks.

Peter and I went out for quite long walks and went out for pub lunches. It was a really lovely time. He and I felt we must make the most of every moment, although I must admit my spirits were high that the operation would be successful. I wrote to everyone we knew who was praying for him, to tell them about the operation, so that they would know what they were praying for now, having had the first stage of their prayers answered. When Friday 13th August came, we kept our appointment at Mayday which was quite lengthy. However over the last 10 months we had become quite used to this. They told us at the end that everything was in order, and we were then ready for

Sunday. When we arrived on the ward, on Sunday morning at 10.00 am, which was to be Peter's home for the next three weeks or so, Staff Nurse Martin was on duty. Peter was going to get to know Martin quite well. The reason for going in so early was because Peter was not allowed anything by mouth except water. They did not seem to need us there all day. Peter had a few tests, a few arrangements were made and then we asked if we could go and sit outside in the sun. There was no objection and when it came to lunchtime we asked Martin if we could go home until something was going to happen. He made some phone calls and said we could go home as long as we were back at 7.30 pm and Peter had nothing to eat.

It was marvellous to be able to go home, and they were really surprised to see us. Clare, Jonathan and Paul were there looking after Ken. We all had some lunch, except of course Peter, and we spent the afternoon looking at photos. Peter had a little sleep on the sofa and we returned to Mayday in the evening. Peter was then visited by the surgeon registrar Miss Dympna Kelly who was to assist Mr Ebbs at the operation. She was petite, young, charming, attractive and Irish with long blonde hair. She sat with us and chatted, making sure we knew exactly what was going to happen. I asked her what she would do if she found there was no cancer. Peter said he had felt so well for the last four weeks. She just smiled and said nothing.

Peter did not want me to go in and see him before the operation in the morning, as he thought it might be too emotional, and I agreed. I telephoned at 8.30 am. on Monday just to make sure he had gone to the theatre as arranged. I stayed at home quietly until I thought it would be time for the operation to be over. They had mentioned approximately four or five hours. When I phoned they asked me to give them about one hour to get Peter settled. The operation had just been completed. It was 1.30 pm.

At about 2.30 I arrived at the hospital and waited in the little waiting room outside the Intensive Care Unit. I don't really know how long but it was about an hour, and then a nurse came to tell me that I could go in and sit with Peter. He was strung up to machinery with a blood pressure band on his arm. This worked automatically every few minutes and registered on a screen above his head, as did every other bit of information. He was also receiving oxygen through his nose. He was swathed in a kind of aluminium foil which was to keep his body temperature up. I was amazed how only such a short time after the operation he was trying to talk, and to lift his head up and move.

By the early evening when Paul and Clare came he was talking and praying and thanking God and only complaining slightly of a pain in his back. He was, at that stage, getting an automatic shot of painkiller every few minutes. Miss Kelly told us later that she had never before seen anyone trying to move like Peter so soon after such a major operation. He had one nurse looking after him all the time; this is always the procedure in intensive care. It did not take long to find out that she was a committed Christian attending the Farnley Fellowship. I had only been a few minutes by Peter, just reassuring him and laying my hand gently on him, when Miss Kelly came in and asked if she could speak to me for a moment. I would have been alarmed had it not been for her expression. Her face was smiling and full of joy. She told me that they had done the operation as planned, but when they had reached the place where they expected to find the tumour, it was not there, on the outside. They then proceeded with the operation; as she explained there is only one way to know for certain that there is no cancer, and that is by pathological examination under a microscope. Having removed half the oesophagus and the stomach they again examined the inside of the oesophagus, and could only see normal flesh. She was very excited. Miss Kelly then went over to Peter and told him the news.

Of course, we were overjoyed, but in a way this confirmed what Peter and I had already been thinking and feeling. Miss Kelly said that anyway everything had gone to the path lab and that we would have to wait about a week for the results. In actual fact it was nine days because the following Monday was bank holiday, and the path lab closed down. When the results came through on the Tuesday 24th August Mr Ebbs sent them back for a double check so we did not hear the final results until the 25th August ...NO CANCER, AND NO SIGN THAT CANCER HAD EVER BEEN IN THE OESOPHAGUS.

It was so wonderful. I felt in my whole being that this was the answer to all the hundreds of people praying across the world. I also had prayed for Peter so much, every day for almost a year. I had laid my hands on him, even at night when he was asleep. I had given him communion every day that he was not able to get to Mass, and Abbot Andrew the Abbot of Pecos in New Mexico, where I had carried out the course on Spiritual Direction just the year before, had helped me with a very positive attitude to pray for the healing of cancer. Many people including Ken and myself and some of the prayer group had been praying the Novena for the canonisation of Cardinal Newman for Peter's intention. Miss Kelly was fairly guarded at first. However she did say that she had never known this to happen with an adeno-carcinoma, as it grew quickly and could not be got rid of with chemotherapy. The chemotherapy was thought to be only a means of shrinking the tumour. Three weeks later as Peter was released from hospital, and after she had had several long chats with him, Miss Kelly agreed to sign a statement. It was obvious to us that she also believed in prayer but could only say officially that the tumour had been healed by non-medical means. Mr Ebbs, although delighted, found it difficult to deal with, and allowed Miss Kelly to cope with the details. During Peter's recovery Miss Kelly spoke of Peter as her perfect patient. She was the one who did the daily ward rounds with her entourage of doctors, and Peter was of great interest.

Peter was in hospital until the 6th September. His recovery to this stage had been amazing. When the significant 8th day after the operation arrived, I was able to take him down to the X-ray department in a wheelchair. He was still very weak and could do very little for himself. A barium swallow was administered to see if the join between the oesophagus and the gut was leak proof. This was 100% successful. What joy! We both praised God and thanked him. We knew that the lady who had occupied the bed before Peter had waited 3 months for her join to be leak proof. Peter was now allowed to drink 30 mls water every hour, and the following day the amount was raised to 60 mls each hour. I made many phone calls, sharing the good news with some of those who were praying for Peter. There was much joyous celebrating.

On the following day 26th August Peter was told he could start eating. They brought him tiny quantities of food, literally half a tablespoonful of dinner with a little milk to drink. He was still being fed through a tube into his intestine, which caused a lot of discomfort. He was told he could eat anything he fancied, but of course he could only manage a minute quantity and had to persevere to get it down. Sometimes he could manage nothing. Some things were easier to swallow than others. I spent my time each day between Ken and Peter preparing food for them both and doing the necessary jobs. We were warned that it could take months before Peter could eat anything like normally. There were colossal difficulties and we tried different methods and listened to many suggestions in order to get some nourishment into him. I kept a diary for three months of every meal that Peter was offered and the quantity that he actually ate. There were some big surprises; egg custard which was for me standard invalid nourishment just would not go down. Small amounts of more crunchy meals were easier.

Towards the end of his time in hospital although making excellent progress medically, Peter became almost depressed and needed stimulating. I felt that this was caused by a process of grieving for his old life. Peter had always enjoyed his food, and the reality of living without a stomach was emotionally painful for him. At this time he could not foresee how normal things were to become. A dietician named Maria gave us both a lesson on 'how to pack his case' properly, meaning how to eat a small amount of very nourishing foods that would keep his diet balanced. Peter seemed not to be interested. I think that he wondered how he would cope with his new regime. However eventually this crisis passed and Peter became peaceful again, looking forward to coming home. As soon as they took away the feeding tube from his intestine he started to feel better, although there was concern that without this food supplement he would lose weight if he was still only able to eat so little and even at times, nothing. Peter found it easier not to try to eat and needed a great deal of encouragement.

On September 4th I arrived home to find that Ken had had a bad fall. He lost his balance while moving his tray from the main table to his small radio table. He felt he could manage it, even though he had promised he would not try and carry it. He had an E shaped cut on his head. He had picked up everything which fortunately had all been closely covered with cling film. The thermos flask was always put separately from the tray. There was quite a lot of blood which he had tried to wipe up. He had sensibly sat down and had a cup of coffee and a cigarette which was a 'cure all' for him. While I had been visiting Father Ken in St Bartholomew's, I had learned that he was quite a heavy smoker. As Patricia and I became more intimately involved with him we both felt that he would have been detoxed, and would not wish to go back to this habit. However, this was not to be. When he was in the Homerton Hospital someone unknown to us had brought him in a packet of cigarettes, which we found in his locker, and they had helped him to smoke one of them. We heard this from another patient as Ken had no idea who this person was. After this, even though he could not manage on his own to smoke a cigarette for many months, or even years, his craving had returned. There was always a fire hazard where he sat, and although we had the carpets treated with protective spray, there were many burn holes around his chair, when he came to live with us

On the night in question, as he began to feel better Ken had eaten his sandwiches. I came in about three quarters of an hour later and immediately called the doctor on the emergency service. She came fairly promptly. She reassured me that the blood was already congealing on the wound and that it would be okay. We cleaned it up and Ken seemed alright. Fortunately he did not seem to suffer a lot of pain from the falls that he had, and was not frightened by them. He took them in his stride. I cancelled his Mass for Sunday morning, but he was determined to go to La Retraite on the Monday. He could see that this helped me while Peter was in hospital. Since Monday the 23rd August he had not been to the convent as the person who took him by car had crashed her car. This was now the third week he had been at home and it was arranged that he would go and return by taxi, trusting that the driver would totally understand his fare and not lose him.

There was an occasion when we had arranged with Ken's brother John that we would put him on the train in Purley, which was then direct to Herne Hill. Ken himself was keen to do this. We arranged with John which carriage and compartment and gave Ken strict instructions not to get off the train until he saw John. We had a phone call from John to say that he had not arrived. We had no idea where Ken had left the train. John was absolutely sure that he was not on it. After the railway and police had been informed Ken was found sitting on East Croydon station, waiting patiently. We went to collect him and decided definitely that leaving him on his own in unfamiliar territory was not to be repeated.

I was a little nervous the day that Peter left hospital. I felt the full responsibility was mine. There were many things that would be easier; I could for instance 'pack his case' better at home. The dietician had said he was to have cream in everything and butter, because more than half of everything he ate would pass right through him, and this extra would give him concentrated nourishment. With Peter at home I seemed to have a little more time. I could attend to some of the letters on my computer, and catch up with Peter's 'story' which Miss Kelly had asked for. I sent two copies of the statement with a letter to Miss Kelly, a copy also to Father Mike Gwinnell and Bishop Howard, with a copy of the Novena for Cardinal Newman which many people had been praying, including Father Ken. His commitment to prayer was amazing. I also contacted the organisation monitoring the progress of Cardinal Newman's cause.

Gradually we weaned Peter off sleeping tablets and pain killers and he slowly improved, but remained tired because it was difficult for him to eat enough calories, however hard he tried. Drinking was particularly difficult. Water was impossible; it seemed to form a bubble with surface tension which blocked the oesophagus. We tried many full protein nourishing drinks, but he hated them and could not drink them. We went for little walks each day in the local parks, but then the weather became wet and there was a great deal of flooding. We changed our venue to the many local shopping centres. This in a way was more convenient as there were more places to stop and rest. After a while Christopher and I thought it would be beneficial for Peter's eating progress to take him out to lunch, so that he would feel life could return to normal in some way. We went to the Kingswood Arms, which has always been a favourite place. Peter ordered cold salmon and salad. He ate a minute amount of the salmon and a tiny lettuce leaf. Eating was always accompanied by all sorts of noises. We sat in a corner with Peter on the inside so no one could see or hear. We had been well used to this with Ken anyway and had learnt not to worry or take any notice.

It was a long slow journey of recovery for Peter. The family were all very attentive. Clare and Jonathan invited us all for Christmas, they were already expecting their first baby in May. Christmas for Peter was both a challenge and a struggle, but he was able to rest on the bed when things were difficult for him, or when he was tired. It was at this time that my sister Josie suggested that we join her for a holiday in June in her flat in Spain, which she had been trying to sell for some time. We promised that we would if Peter was well enough to travel.

Early in the New Year Gerry phoned from Ottawa to invite Peter and myself to go to Florida with his family in March to share their holiday condo which they had booked for two weeks. Peter's first and immediate answer was "No, I couldn't possibly manage." However, having slept on it and prayed about it, his attitude completely changed. First thing in the morning he said "Let's go and risk it." It was a wonderful start of really positive thinking and trust.

March came and with some trepidation we set off for Florida. Peter's rehabilitation went forward in leaps and bounds. We discovered that bread of any kind for lunch like sandwiches or burgers were a disaster, but biscuits like Ryvita, in small quantities were very successful, eaten with butter and cheese or small amounts of other protein. We almost always cooked dinner at 'home' in the evening so that I was still able to pack into Peter's meal unseen ingredients which were extra nourishing, unbeknown to him. We were made extremely comfortable as Gerry and Celia insisted we had the major bedroom, which consisted of a large double bathroom and a large dressing room. We had a great deal of fun with our grandsons Peter and Mark who were then aged eight and six years. They were both good conversationalists and could recount in detail the films they had seen and enjoyed, acting out the parts. We also played many of their favourite board games. During the day we relaxed by the pool and Peter even dared to swim. There were two trained staff who looked after the children by the pool with games and competitions, and they even had a supervised sleep over one night so that parents could be free. Peter was really able to rest. He had lost three stones in weight and this I am sure was also adding to his grieving process. He was also very conscious of his scar which went right round his very thin body.

It was on a visit to Sarasota, that Peter had his first ice cream cone. Eating it was a mammoth task as he had not eaten anything between his regular small meals, but we all viewed it as a great healing. He seemed to enjoy it... some of it anyway.

This holiday was a great success with many happy memories, particularly days on the beach and picnicking luxuriously on the picnic tables provided under the trees. We had trips in speed boats and exploratory visits to surrounding areas by car; every day Peter seemed to be so much better. Peter junior and Mark enjoyed eating out in Denny's, which was a stage better than McDonald's, which Peter could not manage at all. Whilst they would eat large quantities of pancakes, sausages and maple syrup, Peter could tuck into an 'oldies' menu, which was half the food for half the price. Just right!! He began at this time to lose some of his guilty feelings for leaving most of his meal. One evening we went to a rather smart beach restaurant on Long Key. We sat outside overlooking the sea, it was very beautiful. Mark was restless and wanted to wander about. When his mother tried to restrain him, the waitress said, "Aw, he's just antsy!" This was quite new to me so I asked what it meant. "Just ants in his pants that's all," came the reply, "antsy!!" I have heard this many times since. We found the restaurant staff in the U.S.A. very tolerant of children.

One day Gerry and Celia left early in the morning to visit Disneyland with the two boys. There was no way at this stage that Peter could have managed it. It gave us the chance to have a really quiet day and a quiet dinner out on our own. We were able to see how wonderful this opportunity to visit Florida had been. We would not have gone without the encouragement and company. We have thanked God many times for our family and how attentive they have all been in looking after us. In June we felt even more daring and travelled to Denia with Josie, to her flat by the sea. With her organising ability and desire to help Peter regain his strength we had a wonderful time, visiting the many beauty spots in the mountains and relaxing on the beach and on the balcony. We wandered round the market buying fruit and vegetables for dinner and meal times became less arduous for Peter. We went out to dinner several times and he was very at ease, eating what he could manage and leaving the rest without much of the guilt which had worried him previously in restaurants.

We all began to see that life could return to normal, or to what we thought of as normal. It was during this summer that Peter made up his mind that instead of following the advice he had received to have six or so small meals each day, he would try and eat three meals normally with a small snack in between. He was very determined and this proved to be the greatest help in returning to a life which fitted in with more normal living. He always had loved his breakfast and he found that an egg, bacon and toast, or bacon, tomato and toast was a wonderful start to his day, followed by a small lunch and then a small dinner in the evening. This was interspersed with drinks of tea and coffee and digestive biscuit snacks. As the weeks and months went on, in an amazing way, he found he could manage a little more at each meal. Gradually he began to put on some weight. He had been told that he would never be able to do this because of the difficulty of eating. After two years or so no one could even notice or believe that Peter was missing vital parts of his digestive system. It is a mystery to this day, nearly eighteen years later that he is so well. We continue to praise and thank God.

Peter resumed his work as soon as he was able, historical research, writing, publishing and giving talks on the subject of transportation in many forms, from England to the Americas in the 17th and 18th centuries. Our travelling abroad without Ken included visits to Maryland for lectures and book signing, followed by a car journey to friends in Connecticut, then on to Ottawa, to stay with Gerry and Celia. Another time we were invited to Los Angeles, where Peter gave a series of lectures for a week on the Queen Mary. We explored the Californian coast from north to south and took in the Grand Canyon. Peter was much in demand. We also took Ken to many places in Europe, both by plane and car. Life was wonderful. We have never stopped praising and thanking God and all the people who prayed, many of whom we did not previously know and still keep in touch.

It was exactly a year after Clare's wedding, when Peter had been in the middle of chemotherapy, that Paul and Jane were married in Cumbria. We were invited to stay in Jane's parent's summer cottage on Crummock Water for two weeks. We travelled up a week before the wedding. There was some apprehension as Clare and Jonathan's baby was due at this time and she was very determined not to miss the wedding. She and Paul had always been close. There were four bedrooms in the cottage. It was arranged that Gerry would have one of them. He flew over alone as Celia was unable to get time off from the school in Ottawa where she was teaching French. Jenny, who is Clare's best friend, stayed in another room. The wedding took place in the 11th century church overlooking Crummock Water, in the most picturesque surroundings. The wonderful reception was in the village hall which had been decorated colourfully and beautifully. After the excellent meal the tables were pulled back and everyone enjoyed dancing in true traditional country style. Many of the guests stayed in the hotel opposite the church, this included Clare and Jonathan. Paul and Jane decided to delay their honeymoon and spend the week with the guests who were staying on. It was at midnight in the hotel when Clare started to have signs that her baby would be born. This turned into another saga as post wedding celebrations were going on in the hotel. Jonathan took her to the hospital at Whitehaven, fifteen miles over the mountains and lanes. The following day they were due to check out of the hotel as it was then fully booked. In the afternoon Clare was sent 'home' as the baby had changed position and the birth was delayed. Fortunately there was room in the cottage for them to stay with us. It was a devastating time for her and very worrying for all of us. We were entertaining friends in the afternoon who we had not seen for a long time and who were returning home the following day. Clare was still having her labour pains, but not quite ready to return to the hospital.

It was 2.00 a.m. and we were fast asleep when Jonathan, by arrangement, came into Peter and myself to alert us that Clare's time had come. We dressed quickly and raced after Jonathan in our car. He had studied the map minutely, because the lanes were very dark and the way complex. We had no idea how near Clare was to having the baby as when we got to the car she was tucked up in blankets in the back and Jonathan was at the wheel raring to go. Peter and I waited at the hospital until dawn, snatching what sleep we could in an armchair. There was still no sign of an immediate birth. That day most of the visitors who remained went climbing with Jane and Paul and Jane's father John, who knew every inch of the area, while Peter and I walked round Buttermere Lake as climbing was out of the question for Peter. We spent the day trying to find a place to speak on the mobile phone in order to hear if there was any news from Clare; it was difficult to pick up a signal amongst the hills. Eventually the announcement was made when we were all gathered in a hotel having drinks before dinner. The baby had been born safely after a long and difficult labour. There was a great celebration that night.

Several days later when the three of them returned from the

hospital with no cot or pram, baby Christopher was made comfortable in a drawer, which I had prepared as best I could. The local nurse attended each day and all was well. We all stayed to the end of the second week but I could really sympathise with Clare for the long journey back to the south in the car. I remembered my train journey with our Christopher at nine days old, all those years before in mid winter, from Vienna to Belgrade.

Chapter Seventeen

GO FORTH O CHRISTIAN SOUL

It was June 1996. We drove to Dover very early in the morning, taking with us drinks and a picnic lunch. The car was packed with everything we might need in the caravan which we had rented for two weeks by Lake Garda in Italy. Peter and I took the car on the train from Calais to Bologna. Ken sat in the back of the car with the folding wheelchair in front of the seat to his right, where it just fitted, with a large box beside him full of kitchen items. Because we had to take sheets and pillowcases and towels we had quite a lot of luggage so we had two cases on the roof rack. We travelled across the Channel on the Stena Line which was pleasant and we boarded without too much hanging about. We manoeuvred Ken with difficulty up to the top deck from the parking area with some assistance as were taken in the lift, getting him through crowds of people was never easy. We found a quiet corner to make ourselves comfortable and the picnic lunch was pleasant and successful. We returned to the car as we docked in Calais, but to find the railway station where we had to board the train was quite a trial as it seemed to be badly signposted. Eventually we asked a lady who said "Follow me!" and she took us directly there.

We uncovered and un-strapped the luggage on the roof rack and put it in the back of the car having settled Ken in the 'waiting area' in one of the wheelchairs provided.. The café was not open and the cold wind seemed to blow extra fiercely across Calais. Peter took the car to a numbered queue to await boarding the train. When this was done after waiting another hour or so, the café opened and we had a hot drink and a bite to eat. It was then time for us to board the train, about 5.00 pm.

A compartment on the train was reserved for us but by now Ken was getting fractious. Waiting was always difficult for him. We settled him down with his breviary and explained to him exactly what was happening. Eventually we moved off on our journey across France, Switzerland and Italy. Ken was very irritable and difficult. We took him along to the dining room at about 7.00 pm. but he could not settle and we decided that it would be best if we let him eat first in the compartment and this worked out well. When he had finished his meal we left him while we went to eat. He was by then quite happy and peaceful. I think he was agitated if he felt things were difficult for him, especially if he was tired. It was impossible for him to explain his feelings, his anger flared up quite suddenly without warning.

We had quite a good dinner pleasantly served, but very much on economy lines, very different from the way food had been served when I returned from Belgrade on the 'Orient Express' in 1957. It was enjoyable watching the view and the lights in the darkness. We had previously asked 'le conducteur' who looked after us and the cabins if he would delay making up our bunks until 10 pm. so that we could be there with Ken as he would not understand what had to be done.

Just before 10 pm. We collected Ken and took him to the buffet car for a cup of coffee and when we returned our bunks were made up. The one at the top was very high in the roof and not only did one have to climb to the top of the ladder but it was then necessary to swing across to get on to the bunk. The advantage was a wide shelf behind with all one's necessities. Peter had this place; I had the middle bunk and Ken the very bottom one. Whereas Peter had head room to sit up, neither Ken nor I could. For me it was not important; but we had several difficulties of manipulation both in getting Ken to bed and getting him up in the morning. The main difficulty was his last night- time cigarette. He could not sit on his bunk, and he was unable to keep his balance holding on with one hand with his cigarette in the other, so it became a joint effort between him and me. First lying him on the bunk and getting his trousers off and his pyjamas on, then standing him up and getting his shirt off etc and then holding him while he cleaned his teeth. It was quite hilarious with the movement of the train causing us both to sway about. In the morning the process was reversed, and I found it easiest to wash and shave Ken while he was lying on the bed, and then to practically dress him before he stood up. Strangely he was quite happy to let me do this. During this process Peter was banished to the corridor for lack of room. While we were at breakfast the cabin was returned to normal. Amazingly, we all slept well.

We arrived in Bologna about midday and it did not take us long to retrieve the car. We sat Ken on a seat with the straps of our hand luggage intertwined with his arms for safety. Peter managed to bring the car almost to where Ken was, after we had restored the cases to the roof rack, and so we set off to find Lake Garda. Just shortly out of the town we saw a sign to a restaurant directing us down a country road to the left. We followed the sign for about 3 kilometres and came across a superior place where we were the only customers. We had a pleasant lunch keeping the car in full view through the window so that we did not lose all our possessions. The toilets and cloakrooms in this restaurant were superb. I was able to have a complete wash in a large area with bidet and automatic 'switch on' water, with lots of lovely large lush paper towels. Washing, with Ken lying in the compartment of the train, had been limited.

We arrived at our camp on the shores of the lake in the late afternoon. It was very hot but booking in was quick and efficient and we were taken to the caravan which was large and pleasant. Ken rested on a sun bed while Peter and I unpacked the kitchen gear and made up the beds. I went to the shop and purchased a few things for supper and had a quick look round. The camp was only two years old so although everything was new the trees were not yet grown enough to give a great deal of shade. There were many pretty flowering shrubs and the swimming pool was superb. We soon settled in and found our own way to manage easily... fixing the kitchen window on a string so that we could use it as a hatch to the outside table where we dined at night by candlelight. We sometimes ate out in a restaurant.

Ken was happy just spending the day at the caravan. He loved it. He could not get in and out of the caravan without help but he could walk up and down the patio outside fairly safely on his own yet was restricted from wandering too far because of stony and uneven ground beyond. We were able to leave him for short journeys out to the supermarket and for other shopping. In the afternoon Ken liked nothing better than to lie on the sun bed with the protection of two sun umbrellas with a sheet over him, and have a sleep while we went to the swimming pool. When we returned he would sometimes be awake sitting in his chair reading his 'Office' and I would make tea and cakes for all of us, it was very pleasant. In the mornings I would be up early and either go for a walk along the lakeside or join in the keep fit class.

We had many excursions in the car which were very successful, particularly the trip to Monte Baldo which was wonderful. We took a picnic and found the perfect spot in the nature reserve; there were stunning views high in the mountains east of Lake Garda, up a very winding twisting road. Our Sunday trip to Brescia after Mass was very hot and quiet. We had a really delicious and beautiful lunch in a lovely restaurant near the main square. We all had six or seven lamb chops steaming potato 'bolito', mixed salad, wine and iced mineral water. Ken had a wonderful meringue cake with hot chocolate sauce. Peter and I had fresh forest fruits and ice cream; blackcurrants like small cherries, blueberries, and beautiful fresh raspberries, each one perfectly ripe, yet whole... absolutely delicious.

We spent a whole day in Sermione and had dinner one night by the light of the moon and charming lakeside illumin- ations in Lazise a little town just round the lake from us, Verona was old, beautiful and gracious. Ken, like a child, enjoyed his tea and cake... well, we all did, sitting in the shade in a smart café overlooking the Stadium, which looked very like the Colosseum in Rome. We found the disabled parking area with the aid of a charming police girl, who whistled us down for pretending to be a taxi in a forbidden area!! When she saw the wheelchair she was really helpful.

Our visit to Venice was ambitious. We decided to let Ken walk rather than take the wheelchair from the car, because of the difficulties in the crowds on and off the vaporetti, also negotiating the steps, but it was really too far for him to walk. We started an hour late after a very early arrival because the police moved us on from a place where we had been allotted a disabled bay, which was full, but we were told it would soon be free. In the end we decided to put the car in the ordinary car park, very successfully. We sat Ken in a shady place while we waited and he was fine. We then took the No 1 vaporetto down the Grand Canal to St Mark's. It stopped well short of its previously scheduled place as they were carrying out repairs and we had to push through the crowds with Ken walking, it wasn't easy for him or us, we practically carried him. When we reached St Mark's Square there was a long queue of about 200 people, waiting to get into the Cathedral, moving slowly. With many 'permessos' and 'scusis' we pushed and pulled Ken up the queue and into the Blessed Sacrament Chapel where he wanted to be left for one hour. Nobody stopped us. It was sad to see St Mark's so changed. It was roped off allowing only a narrow place for visitors to walk in a queue. However, still no one challenged us even though we sat Ken in an area that was roped off. We had a quick reminder of the inside beauty of the Cathedral and then hurried off to investigate a restaurant for lunch and the vaporetto to the Lido. This would be a little nostalgic trip for us remembering happy times from the past.

We collected Ken by entering St Mark's via the exit and so avoiding the queue, still about 200 people, and again no one questioned us. We rescued Ken and pushed and pulled him, practically carrying him along to a little restaurant.

We went to the Lido on the big boat and Ken was quite okay. On the Lido we took the bus to the Excelsior where we sat on the terrace and admired the view, eventually moving down to the beach bar for tea, exquisitely served by a waiter. Ken had two French pastries and an ice cream and tea. Our neighbours at the next table were Sean Connery and his wife. The Excelsior was the same; nothing seemed to have changed except automatic doors had replaced the older ones. Peter and I reminisced about old times in the Excelsior during the Film Festival, and our 'own' beach hut. Although we had visited Venice several times since then, we had not crossed to the Lido. We made full use of the immaculate cloakroom and were relieved that we could afford the bill for tea.

Ken met a seminary student in the quiet park where we left him while we collected the car; Worlwoff was his Christian name. Ken thought at first that he was a priest as he looked like one, and dared to speak to him. He was Polish and was studying in a seminary in Poland. He had been visiting Rome for a while and was waiting for a bus to take him back to Poland. He had 4 hours to spare to see Venice. Worlwoff's Italian was good but his English was poor, so when I collected Ken I took him to the car to meet Peter so that he could translate for Ken and me. We were always pleased when Ken made a friend on his own as this was unusual. He found any kind of touristic activity tedious. He was interested only in sitting quietly with his breviary or finding something sweet to eat like cream cakes or ice cream. All our journeys were remembered by Ken through the kind of cake or ice cream he had, for instance, a large meringue in Meiringen in Switzerland, an arabic pastry in Vienna, when we were staying on Lake Fűschl in August; the weather there was so wet and cold we made long trips in the car every day; another time he enjoyed a very large ice cream sundae in the Eagle's Nest, the tea room built as a gift for Hitler in 1937 above his house the Berghof. That year we had a hair-raising drive in a bus to the top, a walk through an arch to the original very large brass lift, and so up to the peak, with wonderful views on a fine day across the Obersalzberg.

We had been home for about two months after our caravan holiday on Lake Garda when tragedy struck for Ken. It was Wednesday 21st August. He came downstairs crying and weak. He could not walk properly or use his left hand. I helped him with everything, and when he had settled down I called the doctor as quickly as I could. As I helped him to go back upstairs to dress him in his room he said, "Do you think I have had a stroke?" The duty doctor was Dr Lindsay who we did not know. She was very pleasant and seemed to understand. She was really lovely and understanding with Ken and he responded. She said he might have had a bad fit or a stroke and 24 hours would tell the difference. She said she would return in the morning. We had some difficulty in looking after Ken during the day. By the evening he could not walk or lift his left hand.

Peter and I had a difficult job to get him to the toilet and generally look after him. We managed to get him into bed. It was really difficult to move him. He had put on five stones since the time when I could lift him on my own. In the morning I washed him and shaved him in his room, and only managed to partly dress him, he did not want to be left in pyjamas and dressing gown. He was obviously upset for he was very proud of the progress he had made previously.

When the doctor came about 11.15 am she said it looked as if it was a stroke. Ken's speech had deteriorated and he had become totally paralysed down his left side. Canon Jim Pannett, our new Parish Priest who was in the seminary with Ken many years ago, came and anointed him and gave him Communion. The doctor called an ambulance and I quickly gathered all I thought would be needed for Ken in the hospital. The ambulance station phoned almost immediately to say they were on their way. I went with Ken in the ambulance and Peter followed in the car. Ken was very quiet and very upset. He was understandably apprehensive about what would happen to him. We were taken straight into casualty and Ken was examined by many doctors, and hundreds of questions were asked which I had to answer, as Ken anyway did not remember his own history. A brain scan was then promised. We were there a long time and no food or drink was offered. Eventually I managed to get some sandwiches. One of the doctors who attended Ken knew him; she was a Catholic and had attended his Mass at 12.00 noon on Sundays at Purley. She said "Hello Father Bell" as soon as she saw him; this cheered him up a bit. Sister Sheila was there from Coloma who also knew him and spoke to him.

The brain scan was carried out and then they spent a long time trying to get his original scan from the London Hospital, which was the last one that had been done. Then they thought they might send him to Atkinson Morley. They eventually decided that there was a leakage of blood into his brain that might be seeping. It was in fact a stroke. It was a long day for Ken and for all of us. It was 9.45 when we went with him to Duppas 1 ward; there was no room at Atkinson Morley. Ken was quite insecure but we tried our best to comfort him and I also was very upset. The next day I visited Ken at 2.00 pm. when visiting time started. He had a notice 'nil by mouth' over his bed and was complaining loudly that he had had nothing to eat or drink. They had heard him cough, read that his throat was slightly weak and had sent for the speech therapist who was to decide if he could eat and drink or whether he needed a stomach tube.

I, meanwhile had suggested to Ken the reason was that they might be going to give him another scan. He refused to believe this and said they just refused to feed him. They had not explained to him the reason. I asked a nurse for the reason and she said the Sister would see me. I waited until 3.45 for the Sister. She explained that they were afraid he would choke. I said he wouldn't as he had already had a sandwich the evening before. She then said if I took complete responsibility for him she would give him a drink and something to eat, so I told her that I would take responsibility. They gave him a drink of water, and watched him. Drinking had always been difficult for him. He was very thirsty and very hungry. I pleaded with the nurse to get his lunch but there was no lunch, all they had was bread and butter. That was not enough as he needed protein, he had eaten only a piece of toast and a sandwich the day before with a cup of tea and some water. He was hungry and very verbal about it. I gave the nurse £10.00 and asked her to go to the café on the other side of the hospital and get something. She went immediately and came back after 15 minutes with a ham and cheese and salad sandwich which Ken rapidly demolished.

That night at 6.00 pm he was moved to Selhurst 2 and was completely disorientated, because of all the changes and difficulties, and also was quite unable to move his body. He was shouting a lot, and upset several people in the ward. One man knew he was a priest, because he was a Catholic, and said he shouldn't be behaving like that if he was a priest. I tried to explain, and tried to settle Ken. I think they gave him a tranquilliser in the end.

He was very unhappy and depressed in the hospital. By the end of September he still could not understand that he was not able to walk. He kept falling. They tried to restrain him, but they were not by law allowed to do that. They were very anxious to have him moved as he was causing a lot of upset in the night, shouting and out of control. All thought of extra help for him had vanished when the history of his accident became known.

We were busy seeing social workers and helpers, who gave us a list of Nursing Homes. I visited some and they were quite unsuitable. I was worried and concerned but then Canon Jim suggested Wickham Court Nursing Home, which had previously been the Coloma teacher training college. It had been transformed into a Nursing Home about two years before. After this everything seemed to fall into place. Peter and I went to see them, and after sorting out the finances, on Friday 4th October we moved him in by ambulance. He was able go to Mass and Communion each day as there was a chaplain; this certainly seemed a positive move. Jo Cornish the matron said he could have egg and bacon whenever he wanted it, as this was his favourite and she arranged it for his supper the first night.

Ken was in a room on the first floor and people most probably thought he understood more than he did. One of the staff had evidently been talking with him and could not understand why he was asking for his Mummy although I had already explained when he was admitted to the nursing home that he always called me Mummy. This nurse said "Your Mummy is dead." When Ken said 'What about Daddy?" she said that his Daddy was dead as well. I had been visiting Ken each day and on that Sunday afternoon Clare came with me. We found him in a state of tears and great distress. We could not understand for some time what was upsetting him because his speech had deteriorated. He was clinging to me and crying. Eventually it transpired what had happened and he thought Peter and I had been killed in a car crash.

There were many difficulties to overcome, not the least that Ken still thought that he could walk. No amount of explaining helped him; each time he got up from his chair he fell and he was moved from the first floor to the ground floor in case he fell down the stairs but they were unable to restrain him as it was against the law. He suffered broken bones and many lacerations before he eventually had a series of small strokes which solved the problem as he then could not get out of his chair on his own. This was a real blessing for himself and for everyone else. Another difficulty was his desire to smoke in his own room. The matron had charge of his cigarettes but he would stagger round his room looking everywhere for them. For safety reason smoking was only allowed in the entrance hall which had a tiled floor. After many weeks he was trained to smoke just one cigarette after meals or with a cup of coffee which simplified things. The biggest difficulty was keeping his front clean. At mealtimes this was closely surpervised but the constant dribbling had worsened with his stroke and was made worse if he had coffee and biscuits in his room or even ate a sweet.

I started taking Ken out in the wheelchair to a nearby farm to see the horses which were stabled there and we would sit in the field with an afternoon picnic. If I held him tightly on his weak side he could walk short distances especially where it was flat in front of the stables. He enjoyed these outings and could have a quiet cigarette with a cup of tea from the thermos. I would take a picnic stool for myself and we would sit and chat and look at the view. As it got colder I would wrap him in a blanket and he would wear his Rusian fur hat. We even went in the snow which came early that year. Peter would sometimes come with us and although Ken enjoyed the outings he was still very unhappy and wanted to come home.

One afternoon the farmer who owned the land and the stables stopped us and said we could no longer have access to his farm. He was afraid that I might have an accident with Ken and that he would be held responsible. I was upset as these afternoons had been therapeutic, most probably for both of us. We then started going down the hill to the churchyard where there was an open view of the countryside but in the snow and ice it was very difficult to get back up the hill. Eventually we waited until the spring when we resumed our picnics in the nursing home gardens.

This was a time of a great breakthrough except for the amount of falls Ken was having, things had changed. Jo the matron started surpervising Ken herself. She went to West Wickham and bought two plastic cook's aprons which Ken loved. They were green with a flock of white sheep grazing on them. They could be easily washed or wiped clean and dried. Jo became a good friend to him and his attitude to being there took on a new impetus. He began to appreciate being taken to Mass every day in the chapel and with the constant falls ending everything became more peaceful.

I became known to the staff as Mummy and many of the other patients wondered what my relationship with Ken was as they knew I had a husband. Ken would hold his breviary and look as if he was reading it. We never knew quite how much he understood from it but he found great consolation in holding it and praying, even if he was sometimes in the wrong place or that it was upside down. Some people who had been visiting gave up at this stage, but there were many who had persevered through the difficulties and remained loyal and loving. One of these was his cousin Leslie, who became ill and confused himself and was taken into care.

Eventually the breviary was left to one side, and when I went to visit in the afternoon, if it was fine, we would go into the garden and find a secluded spot with a bench. I would read evening prayer, with Ken joining in the parts that he knew. We would again sing the hymns that he knew by heart, sometimes only his lips moving. We would have some tea from the thermos and a special cake, and we would chat.

As time went on there were many crises. Ken had several bad chest infections, and was in hospital several times, twice to have a cancerous growth removed, and another time when he contracted MRSA. In 1999 Ken started to become very gentle, quiet and even amenable. He became unable to express himself clearly, being either unable to remember or to say the right word. He seemed to have had several little strokes. However we managed to have conversations with him and always had a lovely time in the afternoon, chatting, reading his prayers, praying for our families and singing. He continued to enjoy the little picnics during fine weather. Sometimes he was in his own world, thoroughly at peace. He would tell me he had been to a concert in New York and who had conducted it, sometimes even himself, or perhaps he would have been visiting people long since dead. One day he said Paul had been to visit him and how nice it was to see him and hear his news. We knew Paul was in Cumbria, so who that was remained a mystery. Ken was pleased and happy, what a wonderful blessing. George the matron's husband fed Ken his simple supper every evening and saw to the small things he needed. Ken was very fond of him.

As time went on the matron moved him into a room with a special bed and a hoist. She could see that it would gradually get more and more difficult to look after him. He was still dressed every day and taken to the chapel for Mass, where Sister Mary Goretti would keep her loving eye on him. He recognised me when I went into his room but I believe it was more from the sound of my voice than by sight. He was very caring and loving and lost all his sharpness, although occasionally his caustic humour was evident especially with some of the nurses, who always enjoyed it. I always heard the reports from them. Sadly Jo the matron retired, and of course George with her. It was a very sad day for Ken and I know that he missed them both.

It was during the second week in August 2003 that Ken's health really started to deteriorate; the weather was extremely hot. I would go in often to make sure that he had a little drink even just of water. Drinking had always been difficult but now it was really a struggle for him, yet essential. Eating became difficult and even a small piece of his beloved chocolate would linger in his mouth. I would try and feed him with a little ice cream which he seemed to enjoy. It all took so long and I know that the carers found it difficult even to get his crushed tablets and medication into him. As I sat beside him I would say "Do you remember that I love you very much?" and he would say "Mummy," and then his words would become slurred, I could just make out what he would always say..."and I love you too, Mummy." When I kissed him on his forehead, he would take my hand and put it to his lips. How was it possible to explain to anyone who did not believe in God this agape love? A gift from God, which is love without wanting anything in return. I would ask him if he would like some ice cream. "I don't see why not." was his quiet answer. He could just accept it touching his lips.

It was on the 4th September when we started getting calls to come quickly, on that evening our prayer group prayed round Ken's bed. On the 5th September Father Richard the Chaplain anointed Ken, and Sister Mary stayed with us. Ken was deeply asleep and did not really wake again before we left at 6.00pm. Either Peter or I had been with him all the time. I whispered in his ear how much God loved him and how Jesus was waiting for him, and kissed him, but there was no response. We had just arrived home when the phone rang and we were recalled. Peter had wanted to get a copy of the 'Dream of Gerontius' as this was Ken's favourite. We stayed again praying until 10.00 pm. when we quickly went home to have something to eat. Linda, the night nurse in charge, phoned almost immediately and said she thought the time had come. We returned and she offered us two beds in a room nearby, so that we could rest. I was always concerned about Peter getting his rest, but he said it was better we stayed with Ken.

Ken slipped away to the Lord very peacefully at 6 minutes past one a.m. on the 6th September 2003. I kissed his empty shell. We were so pleased to share this moment with him. My grief was mixed with the blessing of knowing that suffering for Ken was at an end. I was brought to my senses by Linda after we had had a quiet moment; I said that I guessed she was used to death. She said "My son died 4 years ago, he was twenty." I said "Was it an accident?" and she replied "No, he was murdered!"

The funeral celebration of Ken's life was wonderful with the Archbishop and the three diocesan bishops, sixty six priests and a packed church. His coffin entered the church to the sound of his favourite music, the last movement of Mahler's 5th symphony, and went out to another favourite, 'Go Forth' from Elgar's 'Dream of Gerontius'.

Praise God.

It was some months later that I wrote the following poem:

GO FORTH 1977-2003

I did not choose to go
I did not know him.
My name was called, Lord,
And all I said was "Yes."

How could I know
You had a plan for me?
For years I had avoided
Disfigurement and pain
And since my mother died
Had shunned all mental strife...
My memories locked in a deep vault.

You called me and I went
With my love, Peter's help.
He understood your call to me.
I went, to what I knew not.
A quick hospital visit to pray
And do your will,
Or so I thought.

Then duty called to foreign places,
With my love, Peter;
One week with him,
Much work and prayer and fun.
'Može, kako ste vi, Gospodja' and more
To remember was good.

But there were wives
With money to spend
From many nations,
With glittered lives,
And inner sorrows, though well hidden.
While men talked of world affairs.

We saw the beauty round us.
I had seen it all before,
A dream, not to be forgotten
By those with hair back combed
And nails of red.

Back home again,
To yet a stronger call,
To go again to Bart's.
This man, a priest I hardly knew,
I had not even liked,
Unconscious motionless
In bed, with eye upturned
And bandaged head.

My love was with me, and we prayed.
So started my daily vigil,
Answering your call.
My tears were not for him,
for Father Ken, not then.

We prayed, and played his favourite music,
But not ours, my love and I
and I would hold his hand
And chat and pray.
But his response was silence
From his lonely place.

It was not his choice.
Nor mine.
Through weeks and months
My prayer, for him and those who came
Brought healing through my tears, for me,
Perhaps to make me ready
For what then I did not know.
To make me ready to love this ugly sight
With shaven head and twisted limbs
And drooling mouth.

As his need grew,
You gave me love for him,
Abundant love, and carried me
As if on magic wings,
To keep my daily vigil
By this injured priest.
It was so easy, so much prayer
So much love for what? I did not know...
That you were teaching me.

It was not hard, for you were there
By empty bed, in empty room,
In silent chapel, you called me on,
It was for you.
I did not need to see the battered face
And shaven head each day
But when I did I knew your peace.
That peace not known in busy streets.

When others came I slipped away,
Until in fear they said "Please stay."
My tears were not for him,
For Father Ken not then.
I said my name to him in greeting,
Questioned him and held his hand,
I read the gospels, brought him news
And then a miracle.
He squeezed my hand, as I spoke to him
Of things he loved.
His favourites not mine.

An ocean flowed, a century passed,
Or so it seemed, and he was moved.
I knew his secret then, the opened eyes.
The touch of hand, when music played,
The lips that spoke a silent au revoir,
Bye - bye as I said that to him.

Few believed my evidence
And so my love and I kept quiet
We did not need to tell.
We followed you, not him,
Until one day he asked for us.
My love and I.
My tears then flowed for him.

He knew your plan,
As silently you touched his broken body
And damaged mind.
I loved him then as I love you Lord,
But still I did not know,
Each day anew, just trust and wait.

And then through miracles too long to tell
We brought him home to us,
To his new home,
Frightened bent and scarred,
And angry too,
To be loved and healed.
It looked to those who saw
As if this battered priest received it all;
But Lord, my love and I know differently.

Your miracles and favours every day
Sustained our love, until now
A quarter century and more has passed
No longer frightened but at peace and gentle too
Our priest, loving and beloved,
Is beautiful with you.

...and this story of family life and love continues later with sadness, grief and joy.

Milton Keynes UK
Ingram Content Group UK Ltd.
UKHW012005080224
437493UK00013B/436